Instant Korean

**How to Express Over 1,000 Different Ideas
With Just 100 Key Words and Phrases**

by Boyé Lafayette De Mente
Revised by Woojoo Kim

D1422110

TUTTLE Publishing

Tokyo | Rutland, Vermont | Singapore

Contents

Preface

The Korean language has a number of characteristics in common with Chinese and Japanese. These characteristics include their grammatical order (subject, object, verb), the lack of articles (a, an, the), and leaving the subject out of sentences when it is understood from the context.

While these grammatical differences may appear to be an obstacle to English speakers, the trick, when first taking up the study and use of the language, is to ignore the grammatical structure and simply use it the way it is supposed to be used. With this approach, the phrases and sentences you use feel just as "normal" as English.

Some 60 percent of the present-day Korean vocabulary consists of words that were originally Chinese. From around 100 B.C. to 300 A.D. the small kingdoms existing on the Korean peninsula were under the suzerainty of China. During that period, the Koreans adopted the Chinese system of writing, and with it, large numbers of Chinese terms.

In the early 1440s, the king of the unified kingdom of Choson (also spelled Chosun) ordered court scholars to create a new, strictly Korean script for writing both the native Korean and imported Chinese words. This new script, called Hangul (Hahn-guhl), was completed in 1446.

But Korea's elite class continued to use the Chinese system of writing up to modern times. Today, the language is still generally written with a combination of Chinese characters and Hangul.

Another important factor in the study and use of Korean is that a growing percentage of the daily vocabulary of Koreans is Koreanized English—that is, English words that have been absorbed into the language and are pronounced as if they were Korean.

Camera, for example, is **kamera** (*kah-may-rah*). Candy is **kaendi** (*kahn-dee*). Jazz is **jaju** (*jah-juu*). Jelly is **chelli** (*chehl-lee*), and so on. In most cases, the Koreanized English words are still recognizable as English.

The English phonetics provided for each Korean word and expression in this book are designed to get as close as possible to the correct pronunciation. As you will see, the pronunciation follows a precise formula which soon becomes familiar. The phonetic versions are hyphenated to make their pronunciation easier. Just pronounce the phonetics as standard English and practice saying them in a smooth, even flow.

The pronunciation of a number of syllables making up the Korean language cannot be reproduced exactly in English phonetics, but since Korean is not tonal (like Chinese) it is generally possible to get close enough to the "correct" pronunciation to be understood.

Koreans are especially tolerant of foreigners who make an effort to speak their language, go out of their way to help them, and do not fault them for speaking with "an accent."

Here are some very important example words to help you get started:

Korea	*Hanguk* (*Hahn-guuk*)	한국
Korean language	*Hanguk mal* (*Hahn-guuk mahl*)	한국말
Korean (language)	*Hanguk-o* (*Hahn-guuk-aw*)	한국어
Korean (person)	*Hanguksaram* (*Hahn-guuk-sah-rahm*)	
	한국사람	
South Korea	*Nam Han* (*Nahm Hahn*)	남한
North Korea	*Puk'an* (*Puuk-ahn*)	북한

The Korean Alphabet, Grammar and Pronunciation Guides

The Korean alphabet consists of 10 vowels and 14 consonants, which are combined to create some 140 syllables, or "building blocks" that make up the language. The building blocks include 11 diphthongs (combinations of vowels and consonants) that are used to represent more complex sounds.

These vowels, consonants, diphthongs and syllables have been rendered into romanized English phonetics by a number of individual scholars as well as by the Cultural Ministry, and there are some differences in them. In 2003, the Korean government issued a new set of rules for transcribing the sounds of the language into Roman letters in an effort to further rationalize the system.

I have made choices from these phonetic versions and added some of my own in an attempt to simplify the pronunciations and still get close enough to the original Korean sounds so that they will be understood.

There are six basic vowels in the Korean alphabet, plus four "y" vowels for a total of ten. Their approximate English sounds are:

A	Ya	O	Yo	O	Yo	U	Yu	U	I
ah	yah	aw	yaw	oh	yoh	uu	yuu	oo	ee

One or more of these 10 basic sounds are used in all of the syllables making up the language.

The diphthongs and their approximate English sounds:

AE	YAE	E	YE	OE	WI	UI	WA	WO	WAE	WE
aa	yay	eh	yeh	oh-eh	wee	we	wah	woh	way	weh

The consonants and their closest English sounds:

k(g)   as the *k* in "king" or the *g* in "guy"*
n   as the *n* in "name"
t(d)   as the *t* in "toy" or the *d* in "day"*
r(l)   as the *r* in "rain" or the *l* in "lily"*
m   as the *m* in "mother"
p(b)   as the *p* in "pin" or the *b* in "book"*
s   as the *s* in "speech"
ng   as the *ng* in "king"
ch(j) as the *j* in "John"*
ch'   as the *ch* in "church"
k'   as the *k* in "kite"
t'   as the *t* in "tank"
p'   as the *p* in "pump"
h   as the *h* in "high"

*The "correct" pronunciation of five of these consonants (**k**, **t**, **r**, **p** and **ch**) is very subtle. To the ears of native English speakers, the **k** sound is closer to **g**, the **t** sound is closer to **d**, the **r** is closer to **l**, the **p** is closer to **b** and the **ch** is best represented by the **j** sound. Koreans who have become fluent in English say there are some sounds in the Korean language that simply cannot be rendered into English phonetics. Fortunately, as with English and other languages, Korean spoken with an "accent" is still understandable.

There are also five "double consonants" (**kk**, **tt**, **pp**, **ss** and **tch**):

kk   as the *k* in "sky" or in "jack"
tt   as the *t* in "stay"
pp   as the *p* in "spy"
ss   as the *ss* in "essential"
tch as the *t* in "tzar"

It is important to stress the pronunciation of consonants at the beginning of words. It is especially important to "hit" the double consonants hard. I have made attempts to account for the double consonants and other features of the language in the phonetics provided for each word and sentence in the book.

Pronunciation Guide for Korean Syllables

To clearly see and hear the repetitions of the 10 vowel sounds in all of the syllables, read the following lines vertically. [About a dozen of these syllables are seldom if ever used.]

A	YA	O	YO	O	YO	U	YU	U	I
ah	yah	aw	yaw	oh	yoh	uu	yuu	oo	ee
GA	**GYA**	**GO**	**GYO**	**GO**	**GYO**	**GU**	**GYU**	**GU**	**GI**
gah	gyah	gaw	gyaw	goh	gyoh	guu	gyuu	goo	ghee
NA	**NYA**	**NO**	**NYO**	**NO**	**NYO**	**NU**	**NYU**	**NU**	**NI**
nah	nyah	naw	nyaw	noh	nyoh	nuu	nyuu	noo	nee
DA	**DYA**	**DO**	**DYO**	**DO**	**DYO**	**DU**	**DYU**	**DU**	**DI**
dah	dyah	daw	dyaw	doh	dyoh	duu	dyuu	doo	dee
LA	**LYA**	**LO**	**LYO**	**LO**	**LYO**	**LU**	**LYU**	**LU**	**LI**
lah	lyah	law	lyaw	loh	lyoh	luu	lyuu	loo	lee
MA	**MYA**	**MO**	**MYO**	**MO**	**MYO**	**MU**	**MYU**	**MU**	**MI**
mah	myah	maw	myaw	moh	myoh	muu	myuu	moo	mee
BA	**BYA**	**BO**	**BYO**	**BO**	**BYO**	**BU**	**BYU**	**BU**	**BI**
bah	byah	baw	byaw	boh	byoh	buu	byuu	byoo	bee

SA	**SYA**	**SO**	**SYO**	**SO**	**SYO**	**SU**	**SYU**	**SU**	**SI**
sah	syah	saw	syaw	soh	syoh	suu	syuu	syoo	she

JA	**JYA**	**JO**	**JYO**	**JO**	**JYO**	**JU**	**JYU**	**JU**	**JI**
jah	jyah	jaw	jyaw	joh	jyoh	juu	jyuu	joo	jee

CHA	**CHYA**	**CHO**	**CHYO**	**CHO**	**CHYO**	**CHU**	**CHYU**	**CHU**	**CHI**
chah	chyah	chuh	chyaw	choh	chyoh	chuu	chyuu	choo	chee

KA	**KYA**	**KO**	**KYO**	**KO**	**KYO**	**KU**	**KYU**	**KU**	**KI**
kah	kyah	kaw	kyaw	koh	kyoh	kuu	kyuu	koo	kee

TA	**TYA**	**TO**	**TYO**	**TO**	**TYO**	**TU**	**TYU**	**TU**	**TI**
tah	tyah	taw	tyaw	toh	tyoh	tuu	tyuu	too	tee

PA	**PYA**	**PO**	**PYO**	**PO**	**PYO**	**PU**	**PYU**	**PU**	**PI**
pah	pyah	paw	pyaw	poh	pyoh	puu	pyuu	poo	pee

HA	**HYA**	**HO**	**HYO**	**HO**	**HYO**	**HU**	**HYU**	**HU**	**HI**
hah	hyah	haw	hyaw	hoh	hyoh	huu	hyuu	hoo	hee

PART 1

Key Words and Expressions

1 **Greetings** *Insa* (Een-sah) 인사

Hello
Good morning
Good afternoon
Good evening
How are you?
How do you do?

All of these greetings are incorporated in a single Korean expression:

Annyong haseyo. *(Ahn-n'yohng hah-say-yoh)*
안녕하세요.

This universal greeting literally means "Are you at peace?" A reply to these greetings, in all cases, may be a repetition of the above phrase preceded by ***ne*** *(naay)*, which means "yes."

Ne, annyong haseyo. *(Naay, ahn-n'nyohng hah-say-yoh)*
안녕하세요.

More formal versions of these greetings are:

Annyong hashimnikka?*(Ahn-n'yohng hah-sheem-nee-kah?)* 안녕하십니까?

Ye, annyong hashimnikka. *(Yay, ahn-n'yohng hah-sheem-nee-kah)* 예, 안녕하십니까.

Nice to meet you.
Mannasu bangapsumnida. *(Mahn-nah-su ban-gahp-sume-nee-dah)* 만나서 반갑습니다.

How are you doing?
Ottoke chinae shimnikka? *(Aht-tah-kay chee-nay sheem-nee-kah?)* 어떻게 지내십니까?

How have you been?
Chal chinae shossoyo? *(Chahl chee-nay shuh-suh-yoh?)* 잘 지내셨어요?

Good morning!
Choeun Achimiyeyo! *(Choh-eun ah-cheem-ee-ye-yoh)* 좋은아침이에요!

More formal version of this greeting:

Choeun Achimimnida! *(Choh-eun ah-cheem-eem-nee-dah)* 좋은아침입니다!

Goodnight.
*Annyong-hi chumuseyo.**
(Ahn-yohng-hee chuu-muu-say-yoh) 안녕히 주무세요.

*The *yo* at the end of so many Korean expressions, including one-word questions or replies, functions as a honorific that makes them polite.

Hello? (on the telephone)
Yoboseyo? *(Yuh-boh-say-yoh?)* 여보세요?

Goodbye (A final farewell, said by the person leaving)

3

*Anyong-hi kyeseyo** (Ahn-n'yohng-he gae-say-yoh)

안녕히 계세요.

*The literal meaning of this phrase is "Stay in peace."

Goodbye! (Said by the person not leaving)

Anyong-hi kaseyo! (Ahn-yohng-he kah-say-yoh)

안녕히 가세요!

Goodbye.

Sugo haseyo. (Suu-go hah-say-yoh) 수고하세요.

*Said by a person leaving a place of work, literally meaning "work hard."

4

See you later *Ddo poepket ssumnida*

(Ddoh pep-keht sume-nee-dah) 또 뵙겠습니다

also:

Ddo mannap shida. (Ddoh mahn-nahp she-dah)

또 만납시다.

*Ta nyo o gesst ssumnida.** (Tah n'yoh oh keht sume-nee-dah)

다녀오겠습니다.

*Literally, "I will return," said by the person leaving.

*Ta nyo o seyo.** (Tah n'yoh oh say-yoh) 다녀오세요.

*Literally, "Please return," said by the person not leaving.

Please Chom *(Choam)*/Chebal *(Chuh-bahl)*
좀/제발

These Korean equivalents of the English word "please," **chom** and **chebal**, are seldom if ever used alone. The concept of "please" is implied in polite verbs, such as **chushipshio** *(chuu-ship-she-oh)*, which has the meaning of "please do … ."

One moment, please.
Chamshi kidaryo chushipshio.
(Chahms-she kee-dah-rio chuu-ship-she-oh)
잠시 기다려 주십시오.

Less formal:

Just a moment, please.
Chamkkan manyo. (Chahm-kahn mahn-yoh) 잠깐 만요.

Give (it, something) to me, please.
Chuseyo. (Chuu-say-yoh) 주세요.

Please give me some water.
Mul chom chuseyo. (Muhl chome chuu-say-yoh)
물 좀 주세요.

Do (it, something) for me, please.
Hae chuseyo. (Hay chuu-say-yoh) 해 주세요.

Please be quiet.
Chojonghi hae chuseyo. (Choh-johng-hee hay chuu-say-yoh)
조용히 해 주세요.

Please take me to Seoul.
Seoulro ka chuseyo. (Soh-uhl-ro kah chuu-say-yoh)
서울로 가 주세요.

Thank you *Kamsahamnida*
(Kahm-sah-hahm-nee-dah) 감사합니다

also:
Komapsumnida *(Koh-mahp-sume-nee-dah)* 고맙습니다

Thank you very much.
Chungmal komapsumnida. *(Chung-mahl koh-mahp-suhm-nee-dah)* 정말 고맙습니다.

Thank you very much.
Daedan hi kamsa hamnida. *(Day-dahn he kahm-sah hahm-nee-dah)* 대단히 감사합니다.

You're welcome.
Aniyeyo.* *(Ah-ni-yay-yoh)* 아니에요.

*Literally, "It's nothing."

Chon maneyo.* *(Chone mahn-eh-yoh)* 천만에요.

*Literally, "Don't mention it."

Byolmalssumulyo.* *(Byol-mal-ssum-muhl-yoh)*
별말씀을요.

*Literally, "Don't mention it, it's my pleasure."

Goenchanayo.* *(Goehn-chahn-ah-yoh)* 괜찮아요.

*Literally, "That's all right."

7 Excuse me Sil lye hamnida
(Sheel lay hahm-nee-dah) 실례합니다

I'm sorry.
Mian hamnida. *(Me-ahn hahm-nee-dah)* 미안합니다.

Choe song hamnida. *(Cho-eh soong hahm-nee-dah)*
죄송합니다.

I'm very sorry.
Chungmal choe song hamnida. *(Chung-mahl cho-eh
soong hahm-nee-dah)* 정말 죄송합니다.

Pardon me.
Choe song hamnida. *(Cho-eh-soong hahm-nee-dah)* 죄
송합니다.

Sorry to disturb you. (When entering an office or home)
Sil lye hamnida. *(Sheel lay hahm-nee-dah)* 실례합니다.

8 I Cho *(Choh)** 저

*In most ordinary sentences the "I" *(Cho)* is left out
because it is understood. "He" and "she" are used only
rarely because they are also generally understood.

I don't know.
Cho-nun morumnida. *(Choh-nuun moh-rume-nee-dah)*
저는 모릅니다.

I think so.
Chodo Kuroke saenggakamnida. *(Choh-doh Kuu-roh-kay
sang-gahk-ham-nee-dah)* 저도 그렇게 생각합니다.

I'm not going.
An ga yo. (Ahn gah-yoh) 안 가요.

I would like to go.
Ka-go shipsumnida. (Kah-go ship-sume-nee-dah)
가고 싶습니다.

I want to go to Seoul.
Seoure ka-go shipoyo. (Soh-uhl kah-go she-poh-yoh)
서울에 가고 싶어요.

I speak a little Korean.
Hangugma-reul chogum hae-yo. (Hahn-guuk-mah-ruhl choh-guhme hay-yoh) 한국말을 조금 해요.

I cannot speak Korean.
Hangugma-reul mot hae-yo. (Hahn-guuk-mah-ruhl mote hay-yoh) 한국말을 못 해요.

9 We Uri *(Uh-ree)* 우리

Shall we go?
Kal kayo? (Kahl kah-yoh?) 갈까요?

We can't go.
Mot kayo. (Maht kah-yoh) 못 가요.

We're not going.
An gayo. (Ahn gah-yoh) 안 가요.

10 Me Chorul *(Choh-ruhl)* 저를

Please help me.
Chorul chom towa chuseyo! (Choh-ruhl choam toh-wah chuu-say-yoh!) 저를 좀 도와 주세요!

11 **My** *Che* (Cheh) 제

My friend is American.
Che chingunun Miguksaramimnida.
(Cheh cheen-guu-nuun Me-guuk-sah-rahm-im-nee-dah)
제 친구는 미국사람입니다.

Where is my room?
Che pangeun odi itchiyo? *(Cheh pahng-uun ah-dee eet-chee-yoh?)* 제 방은 어디 있지요?

What is my room number?
Che pang-un myopon imnikka? *(Cheh pahng-uun m'yah-pahn eem-nee-kah?)* 제 방은 몇 번 입니까?

Here is my address.
Igoshi Che chuso imnida. *(Ee-guh-she Cheh chuu-soh eem-nee-dah)* 이것이 제 주소 입니다.

Where is my brief case?
Che kabang-un odie issumnikka?
(Cheh kah-bahng-uun ah-dee-eh ees-sume-nee-dah?)
제 가방은 어디에 있습니까?

12 **Mine** *Chegot* (Cheh-gute) 제것 (honorific)

It's mine.
Kugosun che go shimnida. *(Kuu-guh-suun cheh-guh sheem-nee-dah)* 그것은 제 것입니다.

That umbrella is mine.
Ku usanun chegoshimnida. *(Kuu uu-sah-nuun cheh-go-sheem-nee-dah)* 그 우산은 제 것입니다.

You *Tangshin* *(Tahng-sheen)** 당신

Where do you live?
Eodi saseyo? (Eh-oh-dee sah-say-yoh?) 어디 사세요?

*Keep in mind that the subject (in this case, you) is normally left out when it is understood.

Where are you going?
Odiro kasaseyo? (Ah-dee-roh kah say-yoh?) 어디로 가세요?

What are you doing now?
Chigum mousul hago kye shimnikka?
(Chee-guhm mwah-suhl hah-go kay sheem-nee-kah?)
지금 무엇을 하고 계십니까?

Are you going?
Kaseyo? (Kah-say-yoh?) 가세요?

May I take a photo of you?
Saijin chom chigodo doelkkayo? (Sigh-jeen chome chee-guh-doh dwayl-kah-yoh?) 사진 좀 찍어도 될까요?

Your(s) *Tangshinui* *(Tahng-sheen-we)** 당신의

Is this yours?
Igosun tanshin-e goshimnika? (Ee-gah-suun than-sheen-eh guh-sheem-nee-kah?) 이것은 당신의 것입니까?

Is this magazine yours?
Igosun tangshin-e chapji imnikka? (Ee-gah-suun tahng-sheen-eh chop-jee eem-nee-kah?) 이것은 당신의 잡지입니까?

Is that book yours?
Ku chaegun tangshin koshimnikka? (Kuu chay-guun tahng-sheen kuh-sheem-nee-kah?) 그 책은 당신 것입니까?

*Keep in mind that the subject (in this case, your(s)) is rarely used in the sentences.

15 He / She / Him / Her *Kunun* (*Kuu-nuun*) 그는

Who is he?
Kunun nugu shimnikka?
(Kuu-nuun nuu-guu sheem-nee-kah?) 그는 누구십니까?

She   *Kuyojanun (kuu-yoe-jah-nuun)* 그 여자는

She (he) is not here.
Yogi an kushimnida. (Yuh-ghee ahn kuu-sheem-nee-dah)
여기 안계십니다.

He   *Kuege (kway-gay)* 그에게;
                kurul (kuu-ruhl) 그를

Please give him the money.
Kuege ton-ul chushipshio. (Kway-gay tone-uhl chuu-ship-she-oh) 그에게 돈을 주십시오.

Her   *Kunyoe-ge (kuun-ywway-guh)* 그녀에게
also:
                Kunnyo-rul (kuun-n'yoe-ruhl) 그녀를

Please give her the book.
Kunyoe-ge ku chaegul chushipshio.
(Kuun-ywway-guh kuu chay-guhl chuu-sheep-she-oh)
그녀에게 그 책을 주십시오.

Sorry to disturb you.
Sil lye hamnida.

Please give her the book.
Kunyoe-ge ku chaegul chushipshio.

Is this yours?
Igosun tanshin-e goshimnika?

Yes, it's mine.
Ne, kugosun che go shimnida.

What's your name?
Irum-i mwo shimnikka?

I tuck my namecard in the book.
Ee reum pyo chek ye neo eossuh yo.

Please give this to her.
Igosul kuyojae-ge chushipshio. (*Ee-guh-suhl kuu-yoh-jay-guh chuu-ship-she-oh*) 이것을 그녀에게 주십시오.

16 Names *Irum* (*Ee-rume*) 이름

What is your name?
Irum-i mwo shimnikka? (*Ee-rume-ee mwah sheem-nee-kah?*) 이름이 무엇입니까?

Irum-I ottoke doeseyo? (*Ee-rume-ee ah-tah-keh doe-say-yoh?*) 이름이 어떻게 되세요?

My name is Boyé.
Che irumeun Boye imnida. (*Cheh-ee-rume-eun Boh-yeh eem-nee-dah*) 제 이름은 보예입니다.

I am Boyé.
Cho-nun Boyé imnida. (*Choh-nuun Boh-yeh eem-nee-dah*) 저는 보예입니다.

What is her name?
Kuyoja-ui irumi mwoshimnikka?
(*Kuu-yoh-jah-we ee-ruum-ee mwah-sheem-nee-kah?*)
그 여자의 이름이 무엇입니까?

Please write down your name and address.
Tangshin-e irumgwa chusorul sso chushipshio.
(*Tahng-sheen-eh ee-ruum-gwah chuu-suh-ruhl ssuh chuu-ship-she-oh*) 당신의 이름과 주소를 써주십시오.

What is the name of that restaurant?
Ku shiktang Irum-i mwo jiyo? (*Kuu sheek-tahng Ee-rume-ee mwoh jee-yoh?*) 그 식당 이름이 뭐 지요?

I forgot the name.
Irum-I giuk an nayo. (*Ee-rume-ee ghee-uhk ahn-na-yoh*)
이름이 기억 안 나요.

17 Family Names *Song* (*Sahng*) 성

What is your family name?
Tangshinui songun muo shimnikka?
(*Tahng-sheen-we suung-guun mwah sheem-nee-kah?*)
당신의 성은 무엇입니까?

My family name is De Mente.
De Mente imnida. (*De Mente eem-nee-dah*) 데 멘테입니다.

How do you spell your family name?
Tangsin-e songul ottoke ssumnikka?
(*Tahng-sheen-ee sahng-ule ah-tah-keh sume-nee-kah?*)
당신의 성을 어떻게 씁니까?

Please write it down.
So juseyo. (*Suu-juu-say-yoh*) 써주세요.

18 Name Card *Myong-ham* (*M'yohng-hahm*) 명함

May I have your card?
Myong-ham han chang chushigesseoyo?
(*M'yohng-ham hahn chahng chuu-she-geh-say-oh-yoh?*)
명함 한 장 주시겠어요?

Here's my name card.
Che myong-ham imnida. (*Cheh m'yohng-ham eem-nee-dah*) 제 명함입니다.

I don't have a name card.
Chonun myong-hami upssumnida. (*Choh-nuun m'yohng-ham-ee up-sume-nee-dah*) 저는 명함이 없습니다.

I'm pleased to meet you.
Choum boepkessumnida.* (*Choh-uhm bep-kay-sume-nee-dah*) 처음 뵙겠습니다.

*Literally, "I'm seeing you for the first time."

I lost that name card.
Ku myong-hamul iloboryossumnida.
(*Kuu m'yohng-ham-uhl eel-uh-buh-ryo-sume-nee-dah*)
그 명함을 잃어버렸습니다.

19 Age *Yonse* (*Yuhn-seh*) 연세; *Nai* (*Nigh*) 나이

How old is your father?
Aboji yonse-ga ottoke doeseyo? (*ah-boh-jee yuhn-she-gah ah-tah-keh doe-say-yoh?*) 아버지 연세가 어떻게 되세요?

How old are you?
Nai-ga ottoke doeseyo? (*Nigh-gah ah-tah-keh doe-say-yoh?*) 나이가 어떻게 되세요?

I am _____ years old.
Chonun _____ sarieo. (*Choh-nuun _____ sah-ree-eh-oh*) 저는 _____ 살이에요.

How old is your daughter / son?
Ddal-e / adul-e naiga ottoke dwaeyo?
(*Ddahl-eh / ah-duhl-eh nigh-gah aht-tuh-kuh dway-yoh?*)
딸의/아들의 나이가 어떻게 돼요?

Family *Kajong* (Kah-juung) 가정;
Kajok (Kah-joak) 가족

father	*aboji* (ah-boh-jee) 아버지
grandfather	*haraboji* (hah-rah-boh-jee) 할아버지
dad	*appa* (ahp-pah) 아빠
mother	*omoni* (oh-moh-nee) 어머니
grandmother	*halmoni* (hahl-moh-nee) 할머니
husband	*nampyon* (nahm-p'yohn) 남편
wife	*anae* (ah-nay) 아내
parents	*pumo* (puu-moh) 부모
granddaughter	*sonnyo* (soan-n'yuh) 손녀
grandson	*sonja* (soan-jah) 손자
uncle	*samchon* (sahm-chuhn) 삼촌
aunt*	*imo* (iee-mo) 이모
cousin	*sachon* (sah- chuhn) 사촌
younger brother	*namdongsaeng* (nahm-dong-sang) 남동생
younger sister	*yodongsaeng* (yuh-dong-sang) 여동생
older brother*	*hyeong* (hyeong) 형, *oppa* (o-pah) 오빠
older sister*	*nuna* (nuu-na) 누나, *eonni* (un-ni) 언니
brothers	*hyeongjae* (hyeong-jeh) 형제
sisters	*chamae* (chah-may) 자매

* In Korea, how you address somebody depends on gender, age, and how well you know the person, who may not necessarily be a blood relative. The first meaning of *hyeong* (hyeong) 형 and *oppa* (o-pah) 오빠 is "brother." Only

males use **hyeong** to call their elder brother, and females use **oppa** for their elder brother. To address an older sister, males use **nuna** (nuu-na) 누나, and females use **eonni** (un-ni) 언니. However, you will find that in Korean dramas, men address other older men, and a young lady, her boyfriend **oppa**, even though they are not related. Koreans view this as a sign of a close relationship and respect. In other words, it is impolite to address others who are older than you only by their names.

This is my husband.
Ibunun chohi nampyonieyo. (*Ee-buu-nuun choh-hee nahm-p'yohn ee-eh-yoh*) 이분은 저희 남편이에요.

This is my younger sister.
Chohi yodongsaengieyo.
(*Choh-hee yuh-dong-sang ee-eh-yoh*) 저희 여동생이에요.

Do you have any brothers or sisters?
Hyeongjae chamaega issuseyo? (*Hyeong-jae chah-mae-gah ee-suu-say-yoh?*) 형제 자매가 있으세요?

oppa!

21   **Children** *Chanyo* (Chahn-yuh) 자녀

daughter	***ddal*** (ddahl) 딸
son	***adul*** (ah-duhl) 아들
grandchildren	***sonju*** (soan-juu) 손주

Do you have any children?
Chanyo-ga issuseyo? (Chah-yuh-gah ee-suu-say-yoh?)
자녀가 있으세요?

How many children do you have?
Chanyo-ga myon-myong iseyo? (Chah-yuh-gah m'yuhn-m'yuhng ee-seh-yoh?) 자녀가 몇 명이세요?

I have one daughter.
Cho egenun ddal hana-ga issumnida.
(Choh eh-geh-nuhn ddahl hah-nah-gah ee-sume-nee-dah)
저에게는 딸 하나가 있습니다.

We don't have any children.
Ajig upssumnida. (Ah-jeeg up-sume-nee-dah)
아직 없습니다.

Do you have grandchildren?
Sonju issu seyo? (Sohn-juu ee-suh-say-yoh?)
손주 있으세요?

22   **Who?** *Nugu* (Nuu-guu) 누구

Who are you?
Nugu shimnikka? (Nuu-guu sheem nee-kah?)
누구 십니까?

Who is that?
Nugujiyo? (Nuu-guu-jee-yoh?) 누구지요?

Who is it?
Nuguseyo? (Nuu-guu-say-yoh?) 누구세요?

Who is that man?
Chobunun nugu shimnikka? (Choh-buu-nuun nuu-guu sheem-nee-kah?) 저분은 누구십니까?

23 What? *Muot (Mwaht)* 무엇

What is this?
Igosun muoshijiyo? (Ee-guh-suun mwah-she-jee-yoh?) 이것은 무엇이지요?

What is that?
Chogosun muoshijiyo? (Choh-guh-suun mwah-she-jee-yoh?) 저것은 무엇이지요?

What is the price?
Olma jiyo? (Ohl-mah jee-yoh?) 얼마지요?

What is your phone number?
Chonhwa bonhoga muoyeyo? (Chune-hwah bahn-hoh-gah mwah-yah-yoh?) 전화번호가 뭐 예요?

What did you say?
Muorago hasyotchiyo? (Mwah-rah-go hah-shoat-chee-yoh?) 뭐 라고 하셨지요?

What does _____ mean?
_____*ga musun ddushieyo?*
(_____ *gah muu-suhn dduu-she eh-yoh?*)
____ 가 무슨 뜻이에요?

What are you doing?
Mwo haseyo? (Mwoh hah-say-yoh?) 뭐 하세요?

What is this called in Korean?
Hangung-mal lo meorago haeyo? *(Hahn-guug-mahl loh mwah-rah-go hay-yoh?)* 한국말로 뭐라고 해요?

24 When? *Onje* *(Ahn-jeh)* 언제?

When?   *Onje?* *(Ahn-jeh?)* 언제?

When shall we leave?
Onje ttonalkkayo? *(Ahn-jeh tohn-ahl-kah-yoh?)*
언제 떠날까요?

When do you have time?
Onje shigan issuseyo? *(Ahn-jeh she-gahn ee-suu-say-yoh?)*
언제 시간 있으세요?

When will it start?
Onje shichak hajiyo? *(Ahn-jeh she-chack hah-jee-yoh?)*
언제 시작하지요?

When will it end (be over)?
Todaeche onje kunnajiyo?
(Toh-day-chee ahn-jeh kuhn-nah-jee-yoh?)
도대체 언제 끝나지요?

When is your birthday?
Saengile onjeyeyo? *(Sang-eel-ee ahn-jeh-ye-yoh?)*
생일이 언제예요?

When is Korean Thanksgiving day?
Hanguk chusoki onjeyeyo? *(Hahn-guuk chuu-soak-ee ahn-jeh-ye-yoh?)* 한국 추석이 언제예요?

When does the bus come?
Bosuga onje wayo? *(Bah-suu-gah ahn-jeh wah-yoh?)*
버스가 언제 와요?

25

Where? (in/to what place)
Odiro (*Ah-dee-ruh*) 어디로

Where are you going?
Odiro kashim nikka? (*Ah-dee-ruh kah-sheem nee-kah?*)
어디로 가십니까?

Where do you want to go?
Odiro kago shipueusseyo? (*Ah-dee-ruh kah-go-ship-eu-say-yoh?*) 어디로 가고 싶으세요?

26

Where? (at what place)
Odiso (*Ah-dee-suh*) 어디서

Where are you from?
Odiso osyotahyo? (*Ah-dee-suh o-shoat-ah-yoh?*)
어디서 오셨어요?

Where do you live?
Odiso salgo kyeshim nikka? (*Ah-dee-suh sahl-go kay-sheem nee-kah?*) 어디서 살고 계십니까?

Where is the station?
Yoki odiso issumnikka? (*Yuhkee ah-dee-suh ees-sume-nee-kah?*) 역이 어디 있습니까?

Where is the bus stop?
Bosu chongnyujangi odiso issoyo?
(*Buh-suu chohng-nyuu-jahn-ghee ah-dee-suh ee-sah-yoh?*)
버스 정류장이 어디 있어요?

Where is Mr. Kim?
Kim sonsaeng nim odi kyeseyo? (*Kim sun-sang neem ah-dee kay-se-yoh?*) 김선생님 어디 계세요?

Where is my son?
Che adul odi issuyo? (Cheh ah-duhl ah-dee ees-su-yoh?)
제 아들 어디 있어요?

Where can I buy a guidebook on Seoul?
Seoul kwangwang annae so-rul odiso sal su issoyo?
*(Seoul kwahn-gwahng ahn-nay suh-ruhl ah-dee-suh sahl suu
ee-suh-yoh?)* 서울 관광 안내서를 어디서 살 수 있어요?

Where can I eat?
Odiso mok ul su issoyo?
(Ah-dee-suh moke-uhl-suu-ee-suh-yoh?)
어디서 먹을 수 있어요?

27 | Why? *Wae (way)* 왜? / *Wae-yo (Way-yoh)* 왜요?

Why not?
Wae an toejiyo? (Way ahn tway-joe?) 왜 안 되지요?

What's the matter?
Wae kuruseyo? (Way kuu-ruh-say-yoh?) 왜 그러세요?

Why do you like Korean food?
Wae hanguk umshikul choahaseyo?
(Way Hahn-guuk uhm-sheek-uhl cho-ah-hah-say-yoh?)
왜 한국음식을 좋아하세요?

28 | How? *Ottoke (Aht-tah-keh)* 어떻게;
Olmana (Ohl-mah-nah) 얼마나

How are you doing?
*Ottoke chinae shimnikka? (Aht-tah-kay chee-nay sheem-
nee-kah?)* 어떻게 지내십니까?

How old are you?
Nai-ga ottoke doeseyo? (*Nigh-gah ah-tah-keh doe-say-yoh?*)
나이가 어떻게 되세요?

How many are there?
Olmana mani issumnikka? (*Ohl-mah-nah mah-nee ee-sume-nee-kah?*) 얼마나 많이 있습니까?

How much do you want?
Olmana piryo hamnikka? (*Ohl-mah-nah pee-rio hahm-nee-kah?*) 얼마나 필요합니까?

How do you say _____?
_____ *rul mworago haeyo?* (_____ *ruhl mwah-rah-go hay-yoh?*) _____ 를 뭐라고 해요?

---

29 This *Igot* (*Ee-gut*) 이것

What is this?
Igotsun muoshimnikka?
(*Ee-gut-suun mwah-sheem-nee-kah?*) 이것은 무엇입니까?

Is this yours?
Igotsun tangshin-e gushimnika? (*Ee-gut-suun tahng-sheen-eh guh-sheem-nee-kah?*) 이것은 당신의 것입니까?

This belongs to me.
Igutsun chegu shimnida.
(*I-gut-suun cheh-guu sheem-nee-dah*) 이것은 제 것입니다.

---

30 That *Ku* (*Kuh*) 그; *Kugot* (*Kuh-gut*) 그것

What is that?
Kugosun muoshijiyo? (*Kuu-guh-suun mwah-she-jee-yoh?*)
그것은 무엇이지요?

Who is that?
Nuguijiyo? (Nuu-gwee-jee-yoh?) 누구지요?

Who is calling (on the phone)?
Nugu shimnikka? (Nuu-guu sheem-nee-kah?) 누구십니까?

31 Which? *Onu* (Ah-nuh) 어느

Which do you like better, tea or coffee?
Cha wa kopi chung onu gosul choahashim nikka?
(Chah wah koh-pee chuung ah-nuh goe-suh choh-ah-hah-sheem nee-kah?) 차와 커피 중 어느 것을 좋아하십니까?

Which one is better?
Onu goshi to choayo? (Ah-nuh guh-shee tuh choh-ah-yoh?)
어느 것이 더 좋아요?

32 Yes / No* *Ye* (Yeh) 예; *Ne* (Neh) 네 / *Anio* (Ah'nyoh) 아니오

"Yes" and "No" are used in Korean very much like they are in English, separately and at the beginning of responses.

Yes, that's right.
Ne, majayo. (Nay, mah-jah-yoh) 네, 맞아요.

No, that's not right
Anio, an guraeyo. (Ah-n'yoh ahn guh-ray-yoh)
아니오, 안 그래요.

33 Go *Ka* (Kah) (Sometimes pronounced as *gah*) 가

I am going.
Ka yo. (Kah yoh) 가요.

I am not going.
An gayo. (Ahn gah-yoh) 안 가요.

OR:

Kaji anayo. (Kah-jee ah-nah-yoh) 가지 않아요.

I can go tomorrow.
Chonun naeil kalsu issoyo. (Choh-nuun nay-eel kahl-suu ee-suh-yoh) 저는 내일 갈 수 있어요.

I can't go.
Mot ka yo. (Maht kah yoh) 못가요.

Let's go.
Kap shida. (Kahp she-dah) 갑시다.

Let's go for a walk.
San chaekaro kapshida. (Sahn chake-ah-roh kahp-she-dah) 산책하러 갑시다.

Where are you going?
Odi kaseyo? (Ah-dee kah-say-yoh?) 어디 가세요?

I want to go to the post office.
Chonun ucheguke kagoshipuyo. (Choh-nuun uu-chay-guuk-eh kah-go-ship-eu-yoh) 저는 우체국에 가고 싶어요.

34 Direction *Panghyan (Pahng-hyahng)* 방향

front	*ap (ahp)* 앞	
back	*dwi (dwe)* 뒤	
right side	*oruntchok (oh-ruhnt-johg)* 오른쪽	
left side	*wentchok (went-johg)* 왼쪽	
top	*wi (we)* 위	
below	*arae (ah-ray)* 아래	

beside	*yup* (*yuhp*) 옆
inside	*an* (*ahn*) 안
within	*sok* (*soak*) 속
outside	*pak* (*pahk*) 밖
between	*sai* (*sah-ee*) 사이
middle	*kaundae* (*kah-unn-day*) 가운데
across	*majunpyon* (*mah-juun-p'yohn*) 맞은 편
around	*chowi* (*chuh-we*) 주위
near	*kuncho* (*kuun-choh*) 근처

Is there a grocery store near here?
I kunchoe shyupomaket issumnikka?
(*Ee kuun-choh-eh shuu-pah-mah-ket-ee e-sume-nee-kah?*)
이 근처에 슈퍼마켓이 있습니까?

There is a pharmacy across the street.
Yakkuken majunpyone issumnida.
(*Yahk-kuuk-eun mah-juun-p'yohn-ee ee-sume-nee-dah*)
약국은 맞은편에 있습니다.

Where is my wallet?
Che chigape odi issoyo? (*Cheh chee-gahp-ee ad-dee ee-suh-yoh?*) 제 지갑이 어디 있어요?

Your cell phone is on the table.
Haendu poneun takcha wie issoyo. (*Hane-duu pohn-eun tahk-chah we-eh ee-suh-yoh*) 핸드폰은 탁자 위에 있어요.

It is snowing outside.
Pake nuni wo yo. (*Pahk-eh nuun-ee wah-yoh*)
밖에 눈이 와요.

Do *Haeyo* (Hay-yoh) 해요

What are you doing now?
Chigum mwo haseyo? (Chee-guhm mwoh hah-say-yoh?)
지금 뭐 하세요?

Doing homework	*Sukje haeyo (Suuk-jay hay-yoh)* 숙제 해요
Doing dishes	*Sulkogi haeyo (Suhl-guh-gee hay-yoh)* 설거지 해요
Studying	*Kongbu haeyo (Kong-buu hay-yoh)* 공부 해요
Working	*Il haeyo (Eel hay-yoh)* 일 해요
Singing	*Norae haeyo (No-ray hay-yoh)* 노래 해요
Shopping	*Syoping haeyo (Shope-peeng hay-yoh)* 쇼핑 해요
Cleaning	*Chongso haeyo (Chohng-soh hay-yoh)* 청소 해요
Cooking	*Yori haeyo (Yoh-ree hay-yoh)* 요리 해요
Playing soccer	*Chukku haeyo (Chuke-kuu hay-yoh)* 축구 해요
Playing basketball	*Nonggu haeyo (Nong-guu hay-yoh)* 농구 해요
Playing baseball	*Yagu haeyo (Yah-guu hay-yoh)* 야구 해요
Exercising	*Undong haeyo (Uhn-dong hay-yoh)* 운동 해요
Taking a walk	*San chaek haeyo (Sahn chake hay-yoh)* 산책 해요

Taking a bath	*Mokyok haeyo*
	(*Moke-yoke hay-yoh*) 목욕 해요
Washing one's face	*Seso haeyo* (*Say-suh hay-yoh*)
	세수 해요
Putting on make-up	*Hwajang haeyo* (*Hwah-jahng*
	hay-yoh) 화장 해요

36 Speak *Marul* (*Mah-ruhl*) 말을 / *Ihae* (*Ee-hay*) 이해

I speak a little Korean.
Hangugma-rul chogum hae-yo.
(*Hahn-guuk-mah-ruhl choh-guhme hay-yoh*)
한국말을 조금 해요.

Please speak slowly.
Chon-chon-hi mal haejuseyo.
(*Chohn-chohn-he mahl-hay juu-say-yoh*)
천천히 말해 주세요.

Please repeat that.
Tashi hanbon malhae juseyo.
(*Tah-shee hahn-bun mahl so-uum-hay juu-say-yoh*)
다시 한 번 말씀 해 주세요.

37 Understand *Ihae* (*Ee-hay*) 이해; *Alda* (*Ahl-dah*) 알다.

Do you understand?
Ihae hasyoteoyo? (*Ee-hay ha-shoat-soh-yoh?*)
이해하셨어요?

Yes, I understand.
Ye, al-ge sseo yo. (*Yeh, ahl-guh soh yoh*) 예, 알겠어요.

I don't understand.
Moruget ssumnida. (Moh-ruu-geht sume-nee-dah)
모르겠습니다.

Please write it down.
I chongie-sseo chuseyo. (Ee chohng-ee-eh say-oh chuu-say-yoh) 이 종이에 써 주세요.

What is this called in Korean?
Hangun mal-lo meorago haeyo? (Hahn-guun mahl-loh mwoh-rah-go hay-yoh?) 한국 말로 뭐라고 해요?

English *Yong-O* (Yuhng-Ah) 영어

Do you speak English?
Yong-O haseyo? (Yuhng-Ah hah-say-yoh?) 영어 하세요?

Do you speak English? [more polite]
Yong-O-rul hashimnikka? (Yuhng-Uh-ruhl hah-sheem-nee-kah?) 영어를 하십니까?

Does anyone speak English?
Yong-O hashinunbun kyeseo? (Yuhng-Ah hah-she-nuhn-boon kay-say-yoh?) 영어 하시는분 계세요?

The Numbers* *Sutcha* (Suut-chah) 숫자

Two sets of numbers are used in Korea. One is based on the native Korean system, and the other is derived from the Chinese system. The Korean system goes up to only 99. From 100 on, only the Chinese system is used.

Generally, the Korean set of numbers is used when counting things in smaller units, like the hours from 1 through 12. However, all minutes are counted with the

Chinese set of numerals. The names of the months also use Chinese numerals (first month = January, second month = February, etc.).

Cardinal Numbers [Chinese]

0	*kong* (kong) 공 / *yong* (yuhng) 영
1	*il* (eel) 일
2	*i* (ee) 이
3	*sam* (sahm) 삼
4	*sa* (sah) 사
5	*o* (oh) 오
6	*yuk* (yuke) 육
7	*chil* (cheel) 칠
8	*p'al* (pahl) 팔
9	*ku* (kuu) 구
10	*sip* (ship) 십
11	*sibil* (she-beel) 십일
12	*sibi* (she-bee) 십이
13	*sipsam* (ship-sahm) 십삼
14	*sipsa* (ship-sah) 십사
15	*sibo* (she-boh) 십오
16	*sipyuk* (ship-yuhk) 십육
17	*sipchil* (ship-cheel) 십칠
18	*sippal* (ship-pahl) 십팔
19	*sipgu* (ship-guu) 십구
20	*isip* (ee-ship) 이십
21	*isibil* (ee-she-beel) 이십일
22	*isibi* (ee-she-bee) 이십이
23	*isipsam* (ee-ship-sam) 이십삼
24	*isipsa* (ee-ship-sah) 이십사
25	*isipo* (ee-she-boh) 이십오
26	*isipyuk* (ee-ship-yuhk) 이십육

27	*isipch'il* (*ee-ship-cheel*) 이십칠
28	*isipp'al* (*ee-ship-pahl*) 이십팔
29	*isipgu* (*ee-ship-guu*) 이십구
30	*samsip* (*sahm-ship*) 삼십
40	*sasip* (*sah-ship*) 사십
50	*osip* (*oh-ship*) 오십
60	*yuksip* (*yuhk-ship*) 육십
70	*ch'ilsip* (*cheel-ship*) 칠십
80	*palsip* (*pahl-ship*) 팔십
90	*kusip* (*kuu-ship*) 구십
100	*baek* (*bake*) 백
101	*baekil* (*bake-eel*) 백일
102	*baeki* (*bake-ee*) 백이
200	*ibaek* (*ee-bake*) 이백
300	*sambaek* (*sahm-bake*) 삼백
400	*sabaek* (*sah-bake*) 사백
1,000	*chon* (*chahn*) 천
10,000	*man* (*mahn*) 만
20,000	*iman* (*ee-mahn*) 이만
30,000	*samman* (*sahm-mahn*) 삼만
40,000	*saman* (*sah-mahn*) 사만
50,000	*oman* (*oh-mahn*) 오만
100,000	*shimman* (*sheem-mahn*) 십만
200,000	*ishimman* (*ee-sheem-mahn*) 이십만
1 million	*paeng man* (*pang-mahn*) 백만

What is the price?
Olma jiyo? (*Ohl-mah jee-yoh?*) 얼마지요?

It is 52,000 won.
Omanichonwon imnida. (*Oh-mahn-ee-chahn-won eem-nee-dah*) 오만 이천원입니다.

Cardinal Numbers [Native Korean]

1	*hana* (hah-nah)	하나
2	*tul* (tuhl)	둘
3	*set* (sate)	셋
4	*net* (nate)	넷
5	*tasot* (tah-sut)	다섯
6	*yosot* (yuh-sut)	여섯
7	*ilgop* (eel-gope)	일곱
8	*yodol* (yuh-duhl)	여덟
9	*ahop* (ah-hap)	아홉
10	*yol* (yuhl)	열
11	*yol-hana* (yuhl-hah-nah)	열하나
12	*yoldul* (yuhl-duhl)	열둘
13	*yol-set* (yuhl-sate)	열셋
14	*yol-net* (yuhl-nate)	열넷
15	*yoldasot* (yuhl-dah-sut)	열다섯
16	*yolyosot* (yuhl-yuh-sut)	열여섯
17	*yorilgop* (yuhl-reel-gupe)	열일곱
18	*yoryodol* (yuhl-ryuh-duhl)	열여덟
19	*yorahop* (yuh-rah-hope)	열아홉
20	*somul* (suh-muhl)	스물
30	*sorun* (suh-ruhn)	서른
40	*mahun* (mah-huhn)	마흔
50	*shwin* (sh-ween)	쉰
60	*yesun* (yeh-suun)	예순
70	*irun* (ee-ruhn)	이른
80	*yodun* (yuu-duhn)	여든
90	*ahun* (ah-huhn)	아흔

How old are you?
Nai-ga ottoke doeseyo? (Nigh-gah ah-tah-keh doe-say-yoh?) 나이가 어떻게 되세요?

I am 24 years old.
Chonun somulne sarieo. *(Choh-nuun suh-muhl-ne sah-ree-eh-oh)* 저는 스물 네살이에요.

Ordinal Numbers [Native Korean]

1st **ch'ot-jjae** *(choat-jay)* 첫째
2nd **tul-jjae** *(tuhl-jay)* 둘째
3rd **se-jjae** *(say-jay)* 세째
4th **ne-jjae** *(nay-jay)* 네째
5th **tasot-jjae** *(tah-sut-jay)* 다섯째
6th **yosot-jjae** *(yaw-sut-jay)* 여섯째
7th **ilgop-jjae** *(eel-gupe-jay)* 일곱째
8th **yodol-jjae** *(yah-duhl-jay)* 여덟째
9th **ohop-jjae** *(oh-hap-jay)* 아홉째
10th **yol-jjae** *(yuhl-jay)* 열째

---

40 Counting *Kyesan* *(Kay-sahn)*

Like Chinese and Japanese, Korean makes use of special "classifiers" or "markers" when counting people and things. The common classifier for people is **saram** *(sah-rahm)*. [An honorific term, **pun** *(poon)*, is used when the occasion calls for it.] When counting people and things up to 100, native Korean numerals may be used. For everything above 100, numerals derived from Chinese are used.

one person **han saram** *(hahn sah-rahm)* 한 사람
two persons **tul saram** *(tuhl sah-rahm)* 두 사람
three persons **se saram** *(sae sah-rahm)* 세 사람
four persons **ne saram** *(nae sah-rahm)* 네 사람
five persons **tasot saram** *(tah-sut sah-rahm)*
다섯 사람

There are well over a dozen classifiers for different kinds and categories of things. But there is also a "universal classifier" — *kae (kay)* — that may be used when one is in doubt about the "correct" one to use. The classifiers come after the appropriate number.

universal classifier	*kae (kay)* 개
classifiers for:	
people	*saram (sah-rahm)* 사람, *myung (mhyung)* 명, *bun (bhun)* 분
glasses, cups of	*jan (jahn)* 잔, *cup (cup)* 컵
animals and fish	*mari (mah-ree)* 마리
books, magazines, notebooks	*kwon (kwahn)* 권
bottles (of beer, water, etc.)	*byong (b'yung)* 병
boxes and packages	*sangja (sang-jah)* 상자, *kap (kahp)* 갑
buildings and houses	*chae (chay)* 채
building floors	*chung (chuung)* 층
cars and other machines	*tae (tay)* 대
paper, bills, tickets, etc.	*jang (jahng)* 장
slender things like pencils, sticks	*charu (chah-ruu)* 자루
bags of	*bongji (bohng-jee)* 봉지
trees	*kuru (kuu-ruu)* 그루
flowers, grapes	*songi (sohng-ee)* 송이
bunches of	*dabal (dah-bahl)* 다발
clothes	*beol (beol)* 벌
pairs of shoes	*kyulre (kyhul-reh)* 켤레
pieces, slices of	*jogak (jo-gahk)* 조각, *chok (choke)* 쪽

bowls of	**geurut** (*gu-rut*) 그릇,
	kongi (*kohng-gee*) 공기
couple, pair	**ssang** (*ssahng*) 쌍

Two sheets of paper, please.
Tu jang juseyo. (*Tuu jahng juu-say-yoh*) 두 장 주세요.

Three tickets, please.
Pyo se jang juseyo. (*P'yoh seh jahng juu-say-yoh*)
표 세 장 주세요.

Two glasses of beer, please.
Maekchu tu jan juseyo. (*Make-juu tuu jahn juu-say-yoh*)
맥주 두 잔 주세요.

Two bottles of beer, please.
Maekchu tu byong, juseyo. (*Make-juu tuu b'yung, juu-say-yoh*) 맥주 두 병 주세요.

One flower, please.
Kot han songi, juseyo. (*Kaht han shong-ee, juu-say-yoh*)
꽃 한 송이 주세요.

The US embassy is located on the first floor of this building.
Miguk taesagwanen ibuilding ilchunge issuyo. (*Mee-guuk tay-sah-gwahn-eun ee-building eel-chuung-ee ees-suh-yoh*)
미국 대사관은 이 빌딩 일층에 있어요.

What floor?
Myot change? (*M'yaht chuung?*) 몇 층?

I have four cats.
Chonun koyangega ne mari isseoyo.
(*Choh-nuun koh-yahng-ee-gah nay mah-ree ee-sah-yoh*)
저는 고양이가 네마리 있어요.

How many books do you need?
Chaeki myo kwon piryo haseyo? (*Chake-ee m'yoe kwahn pee-rio hah-say-yoh?*) 책이 몇 권 필요하세요?

41 Time

(In the sense of hours)	*Shigan* (*She-gahn*) 시간
(As in period of time)	*Kigan* (*Kee-gahn*) 기간
minute	*pun* (*poon*) 분 or *bun* (*boon*) 분
hour	*shigan* (*she-gahn*) 시간
o'clock	*shi* (*she*) 시
a.m.	*ojon* (*oh-jahn*) 오전
p.m.	*ohu* (*oh-huu*) 오후

A combination of Korean and Chinese numbers is used in telling time. The hours are expressed in native Korean numbers, some of which are abbreviated. Minutes are expressed in numbers derived from Chinese.

1 o'clock	*han shi* (*hahn she*) 한 시
2 o'clock	*tu shi* (*tuu she*) 두 시
3 o'clock	*se shi* (*say she*) 세 시
4 o'clock	*ne shi* (*nay she*) 네 시
5 o'clock	*tasot shi* (*tah-sut she*) 다섯 시
6 o'clock	*yosot shi* (*yuu-sut she*) 여섯 시
7 o'clock	*ilgop shi* (*eel-gupe she*) 일곱 시
8 o'clock	*yodol shi* (*yoh-dahl she*) 여덟 시
9 o'clock	*ahop shi* (*ah-hope she*) 아홉 시
10 o'clock	*yol shi* (*yohl she*) 열 시
11 o'clock	*yolhan shi* (*yohl-hahn she*) 열한 시
12 o'clock	*yolttu shi* (*yohl-duu she*) 열두 시

Minutes are expressed using adapted Chinese numbers:

1 minute	*il bun* *(eel boon)*	일 분
2 minutes	*i bun* *(ee boon)*	이 분
3 minutes	*sam bun* *(sahm boon)*	삼 분
4 minutes	*sa bun* *(sah boon)*	사 분
5 minutes	*o bun* *(oh boon)*	오 분
6 minutes	*yuk ppun* *(yuhk poon)*	육 분
7 minutes	*ch'il bun* *(cheel boon)*	칠 분
8 minutes	*p'al bun* *(pahl boon)*	팔 분
9 minutes	*ku bun* *(kuu boon)*	구 분
10 minutes	*ship ppun* *(ship poon)*	십 분
11 minutes	*ship-il bun* *(ship-eel boon)*	십일 분
12 minutes	*ship-i bun* *(ship-ee boon)*	십이 분
13 minutes	*ship-sam bun* *(ship-sahm boon)*	십삼 분
14 minutes	*ship-sa bun* *(ship-sah boon)*	십사 분
15 minutes	*ship-o bun* *(ship-oh boon)*	십오 분
16 minutes	*shim-nyuk ppun* *(sheem-n'yuhk poon)* 십육 분	
17 minutes	*ship-ch'il bun* *(ship-cheel boon)*	십칠 분
18 minutes	*ship-p'al bun* *(ship-pahl boon)*	십팔 분
19 minutes	*ship-kku bun* *(ship-kuu boon)*	십구 분
20 minutes	*i-ship ppun* *(ee-ship poon)*	이십 분
21 minutes	*i-ship-il bun* *(ee-ship-eel boon)*	이십일 분
22 minutes	*i-ship-i bun* *(ee-ship-ee boon)*	이십이 분
23 minutes	*i-ship-sam bun* *(ee-ship-sahm boon)* 이십삼 분	
24 minutes	*i-ship-sa bun* *(ee-ship-sah boon)* 이십사 분	
25 minutes	*i-ship-o bun* *(ee-ship-oh boon)*	이십오 분
26 minutes	*i-shim-nyuk ppun* *(ee-sheem-n'yuhk poon)* 이십육 분	

27 minutes	*i-ship-ch'il bun* (*ee-ship-cheel boon*)
	이십칠 분
28 minutes	*i-ship-p'al bun* (*ee-ship-pahl boon*)
	이십팔 분
29 minutes	*i-ship-kku bun* (*ee-ship-kuu boon*)
	이십구 분
30 minutes	*sam-ship ppun* (*sahm-ship poon*) 삼십 분
40 minutes	*sa-ship ppun* (*sah-ship poon*) 사십 분
50 minutes	*o-ship ppun* (*oh-ship poon*) 오십 분
51 minutes	*o-ship-il bun* (*oh-ship-eel boon*) 오십일 분
52 minutes	*o-ship-i bun* (*oh-ship-ee boon*) 오십이 분
53 minutes	*o-ship-sam bun* (*oh-ship-sahm boon*)
	오십삼 분
54 minutes	*o-ship-sa bun* (*oh-ship-sah boon*)
	오십사 분
55 minutes	*o-ship-o bun* (*oh-ship-oh boon*) 오십오 분

What time is it?
Myot shi imnikka? (*M'yaht she eem-nee-kkah?*)
몇 시입니까?

It's 4 o'clock.
Ne shi yeyo. (*Nay she yay-yoh*) 네시예요.

It's 4:30.
Ne shi pan. (*Nay she pahn*) 네 시 반.

Five minutes after four.
Ne shi obun. (*Nay she oh-boon*) 네 시 오 분.

Fifteen minutes after five.
Tasot shi shibo bun. (*Tah-saht she she-boh boon*)
다섯시 십오분.

Designations for a.m. and p.m. are placed before the hour, as in:

It is 12 p.m.
Ohu yoltu shi imnida. *(Oh-huu yahl-tuu she eem-nee-dah)*
오후 열두시 입니다.

It's 6:30 p.m.
Ohu yasot shi samship pun. *(Oh-huu yah-saht she sahm-ship poon)* 오후 여섯시 삼십분.

It's 6:30 a.m.
Ojon yasot shi samship pun. *(Oh-joan yah-saht she sahm-ship poon)* 오전 여섯시 삼십분.

night	*pam* *(pahm)* 밤;
	yagan *(yah-gahn)* 야간
at night	*pame* *(pah-may)* 밤에
all night/ overnight	*pamsaedorok* *(pahm-say-doh-roak)* 밤새도록
every night	*pammada* *(pahm-mah-dah)* 밤마다
tonight	*onul chonyok* *(oh-nuhl chun-yuk)* 오늘 저녁
last night	*kanbam* *(kahn-bahm)* 간밤
tomorrow	*naeil* *(nay-eel)* 내일
tomorrow morning	*naeil achim* *(nay-eel ah-cheem)* 내일 아침
tomorrow evening	*naeil chonyok* *(nay-eel chun-yuhk)* 내일 저녁

See you tomorrow.
Naeil poepkessumnida. *(Nay-eel pope-keh-sume-nee-dah)* 내일 뵙겠습니다.

Do you have time tonight?
Onul chonyoke shigan issuseyo? (Oh-nuhl chun-yuk-ee
she-gaahn ee-suu-say-yoh?) 오늘 저녁에 시간 있으세요?

I stayed up all night.
Chuun pamsaedorok jamul mot jatsumnida. (Chu-nuun
pahm-say-doh-roak jahm-uhl mot jat-sum-nee-dah)
저는 밤새도록 잠을 못 잤습니다.

always	*hangsang* (hang-sahng) 항상	
often	*chaju* (chah-juu) 자주	
usually	*botong* (boh-tohng) 보통	
occasionally	*gakkum* (gah-kkum) 가끔	
rarely	*byolro* (b'yohl-roh) 별로	
hardly ever	*kuai* (kuu-ee) 거의	
never	*chon hyo* (chone-h'yoh) 전혀	

I often have Korean food.
Choun chaju hankuk umshikul moksumnida. (Chuh-
nuun chah-juu hahn-guuk-uum-sheek-uhl mokk-sum-nee-dah)
저는 자주 한국 음식을 먹습니다.

I rarely eat out.
Choun byolro oeshikul anhamnida.
(Chuh-nuun b'yol-roh way-sheek-uhl ahn-ham-nee-dah)
저는 별로 외식을 안 합니다.

I am almost done.
Kuai da haessumnida. (Kuu-ee dah hay-sume-nee-dah)
거의 다 했습니다.

---

42 **Days** *Yoil (Yoe-eel)*

Sunday	*Ilyoil* (Eel-yoe-eel) 일요일

Monday	*Wolyoil (Wuhl-yoe-eel)* 월요일	
Tuesday	*Hwayoil (Whah-yoe-eel)* 화요일	
Wednesday	*Suyoil (Suu-yoe-eel)* 수요일	
Thursday	*Mokyoil (Moke-yoe-eel)* 목요일	
Friday	*Kumyoil (Kuhm-yoe-eel)* 금요일	
Saturday	*Toyoil (Toe-yoe-eel)* 토요일	
yesterday	*oje (ah-jay)* 어제	
today	*onul (oh-nuhl)* 오늘	
tomorrow	*naeil (nay-eel)* 내일	
day after tomorrow	*mo-re (moh-reh)* 모레	
day before yesterday	*ku jo ke (kuu joh keh)* 그저께	
early morning	*sae byok (say b'yuk)* 새벽	
morning	*ojon (oh-jahn)* 오전	
afternoon	*ohu (oh-huu)* 오후	

What day is today?
Onu-run musun yoil-i-e yo? (Oh-nuu-ruun muu-suun yohl ee-eh yoh?) 오늘은 무슨 요일이에요?

Today is Wednesday.
Onu-run suyoilimnida. (Oh-nuu-ruun suu-yoe-eel eem-nee-dah) 오늘은 수요일입니다.

What did you do yesterday?
Oje mwo ha-shyeo sseo yo? (Ah-jay mwah hah-shay say-oh yoh?) 어제 뭐 하셨어요?

Let's meet on Thursday at 5 p.m.
Mokyoil ohu tasot shie mannap shida. (Moke-yoe-eel oh-huu tah-sut she-ee mahn-nahp she-dah) 목요일 오후 다섯시에 만납시다.

Counting Days

Days, in smaller numbers, are generally counted using the native Korean set of numerals, with the terms abbreviated.

one day	*haru* (hah-ruu)	하루
two days	*i teul* (ee tulh)	이틀
three days	*sa heul* (sah huhl)	사흘
four days	*na heul* (nah huhl)	나흘
five days	*tat sae* (taht say)	닷새
six days	*yot sae* (yaht say)	엿새
seven days	*i re* (ee ray)	이레
eight days	*yodu re* (yah-duh ray)	여드레
nine days	*ahu re* (ah-huu ray)	아흐레
ten days	*yo reul* (yah ruhl)	열흘

I have an engagement ceremony in ten days.

Yo reul duie yakon shiki issumnida. (Yah ruhl dui-ee yah-kohn sheek-eh e-sume-nee-dah) 열흘 뒤에 약혼식이 있습니다.

Shall we meet two days later?

I teul duie mannalkkayo? (Ee-tuhl dui- eh mahn-nahl-kah-yoh?) 이틀 뒤에 만날까요?

Weeks *Chu* (Chuu) 주

a week's time	*chugan* (chuu-gahn)	주간
this week	*ibon chu* (ee-bohn chuu)	이번 주
last week	*chinan ju* (chee-nahn juu)	지난 주
next week	*taum chu* (tah-uum chuu)	다음 주
every week	*mae ju* (may juu)	매 주

| weekday | *pyongil* *(p'yohng-eel)* 평일 |
| weekend | *chumal* *(chuu-mahl)* 주말 |

Do you have time this week Friday?
Ibon chu Kumyoile shigan issuseyo?
(Ee-bohn chuu kuhm-yoe-eel-eh she-gahn ee-suu-say-yoh?)
이번 주 금요일에 시간 있으세요?

I am busy during the weekdays.
Choun pyongilenun babbah yo. *(Choh-nuun p'yohng-eel-eh-nuun bah-bbah yoh)* 저는 평일에는 바빠요.

There will be a Korean festival on next weekend.
Taum chumale hanguk chukchega issumnida.
(Tah-uum chuu-mahl-eh hahn-gukk chuuk-chuh-gah issum-nee-dah) 다음 주말에 한국 축제가 있습니다.

45 Counting Weeks

Weeks are normally counted using the Chinese set of numbers.

one week	*il chuil* *(eel juu-eel)* 일주일
two weeks	*i chuil* *(ee juu-eel)* 이주일
three weeks	*sam chuil* *(sahm juu-eel)* 삼주일
four weeks	*sa chuil* *(sah juu-eel)* 사주일
five weeks	*o chuil* *(oh juu-eel)* 오주일
six weeks	*yuk chuil* *(yuuk juu-eel)* 육주일
seven weeks	*chil juil* *(cheel juu-eel)* 칠주일
eight weeks	*pal juil* *(pahl juu-eel)* 팔주일
nine weeks	*ku chuil* *(kuu juu-eel)* 구주일
ten weeks	*ship chuil* *(ship juu-eel)* 십주일

Months *Wol* (Wahl) 월

The terms for the months are combinations of the Chinese numbers 1 through 12, plus *wol* (wahl) for "month." *Tal* (tahl) is another word for "month."

January	*Irwol* (Eer-wuhl) 일월
February	*Iwol* (Ee-wuhl) 이월
March	*Samwol* (Sahm-wuhl) 삼월
April	*Sawol* (Sah-wuhl) 사월
May	*Owol* (Oh-wuhl) 오월
June	*Yuwol* (Yuu-wuhl) 유월
July	*Chilwol* (Cheel-wuhl) 칠월
August	*Palwol* (Pahl-wuhl) 팔월
September	*Kuwol* (Kuu-wuhl) 구월
October	*Shiwol* (She-wuhl) 시월
November	*Shibilwol* (She-beel-wuhl) 십일월
December	*Shibiwol* (She-bee-wuhl) 십이월
this month	*i dal* (ee dahl) 이달
last month	*chinan dal* (chee-nahn dahl) 지난달
next month	*taum tal* (tah-uum dahl) 다음달
one month	*han tal* (hahn dahl) 한달

When is your birthday?
Saeng-iri onje eyo? (Sang-ee-ree uhn-jeh eh-yoh?)
생일이 언제예요?

My birthday is on June 3.
Che saeng-iren yuwol samil imnida. (Cheh sang-il-en yuu-wuhl sahm-il eem-nee-dah) 제 생일은 유월 삼일입니다.

What day is Hangul Lal?
Hangul Lali myotwol myochil imnikka?
(Hahn-guhl Lahl-ee mwuht-wol-myo-chil mm-nee-kah?)
한글날이 몇 월 며칠 입니까?

Hangul Lal is on October 9.
Hangul Lalen shiwol kuil imnida. (Hangul Lal-en she-wuhl-ky-il eem-nee-dah) 한글날은 시월 구일입니다.

47 Years *Hae (Hay)* 해

Nyon (N'yuhn) – when in compounds

this year	*al hae (al-hay)* 올해
next year	*nae nyon (nay n'yuhn)* 내년
last year	*chang nyon (chahng n'yuhn)* 작년
every year	*mae nyon (may n'yuhn)* 매년
New Year's Day	*Sol Lal (Sohl Lahl)* 설날
Thanksgiving Day	*Chusok* (Chuu-soak) 추석

I wish you a Happy New Year!
Saehae pok mani padushipshio! (Say-ahy poak mah-nee pah-duh-ship-she-oh) 새해 복 많이 받으세요!

When is the lunar New Year's day this year?
Al hae umryok Sol Lale onje eyo?
(Al-hay umm-r'yuk Sohl Lahl-ee uhn-jeh eh-yoh?)
올해 음력 설날이 언제예요?

What is your (Chinese zodiac) sign?
Musun tiyeyo? (Muu-suun tee-yah-yoh?) 무슨 띠예요?

Counting Years

Years are normally counted with the Chinese set of numerals.

one year	*il nyon* (*eel n'yun*)	일년
two years	*i nyon* (*ee n'yun*)	이년
three years	*sam nyon* (*sahm n'yun*)	삼년
four years	*sa nyon* (*sah n'yun*)	사년
five years	*o nyon* (*oh n'yun*)	오년
six years	*yung nyon* (*young n'yun*)	육년
seven years	*chil nyon* (*cheel n'yun*)	칠년
eight years	*pal nyon* (*pahl n'yun*)	팔년
nine years	*ku nyon* (*kuu n'yun*)	구년
ten years	*shim nyon* (*sheem n'yun*)	십년

Money *Ton* (*Tone*) 돈

money	*ton* (*tone*) 돈	
cash	*hyon gum* (*hyun guhm*) 현금	
credit card	*shinyong kadu* (*sheen-yohng kah-duu*) 신용 카드	
debit card	*hyon Gum kadu* (*hyun Guhm kah-duu*) 현금 카드 / *Jigbul kadu* (*jeeg-buhl kah-duu*) 직불 카드 / *Cheku kadu* (*check kah-duu*) 체크 카드	

Korean currency *won* (*won/wan*). *Won* coins come in four denominations:

10 won	*ship won* (*sheep won*)	십원
50 won	*oship won* (*oh-sheep won*)	오십원
100 won	*paek won* (*bake won*)	백원

500 won	*o-baek won (oh-bake won)* 오백원

Notes or bills come in four denominations:

1,000 won	*chon won (chone won)* 천원
5,000 won	*ochon won (oh-chone won)* 오천원
10,000 won	*man won (mahn won)* 만원
50,000 won	*oman won (oh-mahn won)* 오만원
currency exchange	*hwan jon (wahn jahn)* 환전
exchange rate	*hwanyul (hwahn-yuhl)* 환율
U.S. dollars	*dallo (dahl-lah)* 달러
Japanese yen	*Ilbon en (Eel-bone inn)* 일본 엔
Chinese currency	*Chungguk yuan (Chuung-guuk yu-ahn)* 중국 위엔
travelers' check	*yohangja supyo (yuh-hang-jah supe-yoh-ruhl)* 여행자 수표

How much?
Eol mayeyo? (Eh-ohl mah-yay-oh?) 얼마예요?

I have no cash, can I pay by credit card?
Hyon gumi opnundeyo, shinyong kadu twaeyo? (Hyun guhm-ee ope-nuun-day-yoh sheen-yohng kah-duu t'way-yoh?) 현금이 없는데요 신용카드 돼요?

What is the current exchange rate?
Dalleoeui hwanyuri otteoke twaeyo?
(Dahl-lay-oh-we hwahn-yuu-ree aht-teh-oh-keh t'way-yoh?) 달러의 환율이 어떻게 돼요?

Where can I change money?
Ton-eul odiso pakkweoyo? (Tone-yule ah-dee-soh pahk-kway-oh-yoh?) 돈을 어디서 바꿔요?

Do you accept travelers' checks?
Yohaengja supyo-rul pa ssumnikka? (Yuh-hang-jah suup-yoh-ruhl pah ssume-nee-kah?) 여행자 수표를 받습니까?

Please give me small change for this.
Chan don euro chuseyo. (Chahn doan eh-uu-roh chuu-say-yoh) 잔돈으로 주세요.

50 Seasons *Kyejol* (Kay-juhl) 계절

spring	*pom (pome)* 봄
in spring	*pom e (pome eh)* 봄에
summer	*yorum (yoh-rume)* 여름
in summer	*yorum e (yoh-rume eh)* 여름에
fall	*kaul (kah-uhl)* 가을
in fall	*kaul e (kah-uhl eh)* 가을에
winter	*kyoul (k'yoh-uhl)* 겨울
in winter	*kyoul e (k'yoh-uhl eh)* 겨울에

51 The Weather *Nalsshi* (Nahl-she) 날씨

clouds	*kurum (kuu-ruum)* 구름
wind	*param (pah-rahm)* 바람
rain	*pi (pee)* 비
snow	*nun (nuun)* 눈
snow storm	*nun bora (nuun boh-rah)* 눈보라
typhoon	*taepung (tay-puung)* 태풍
ice	*orum (uu-ruhm)* 얼음; *aesu (aye-suu)* 아이스

overcast	**nalsshiga hurlyoyo** (*nahl-she-gah huu-layoh-yoh*) 날씨가 흐려요
clear	**nalsshiga malgayo** (*nahl-she-gah mahl-gah-yoh*) 날씨가 맑아요
windy	**parami puroyo** (*pah-rah-me puu-ruh-yoh*) 바람이 불어요
rain (verb)	**piga woyo** (*pee-gah wah-yoh*) 비가 와요
snow (verb)	**nuni woyo** (*nuun-ee wah-yoh*) 눈이 와요
cold	**chuwoyo** (*chuu-wah-yoh*) 추워요
chilly	**ssalssalhaeyo** (*ssahl-ssahl-hay-yoh*) 쌀쌀해요
cool	**sonurhaeyo** (*suh-nur-hay-yoh*) 서늘해요
hot	**towoyo** (*tah-wah-yoh*) 더워요
warm	**ddattutaeyo** (*ddaht-tuh-tay-yoh*) 따뜻해요

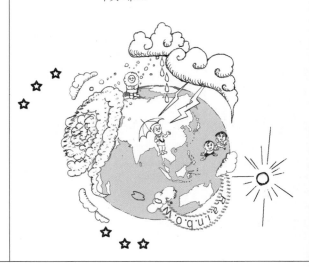

How is the weather today?
Onul nalssinun otto ssumnikka? (*Oh-nuhl nahl-she-nuun aht-toh sume-nee-kah?*) 오늘 날씨는 이떻습니까?

OR:

Onul nalssiga otteyo? (*Oh-nuhl nahl-she-gah aht-tay-yoh?*) 오늘 날씨가 어때요?

It looks like rain, doesn't it?
Pi ga ol kot katchiyo? (*Pee gah ohl kaht kaht-chee-yoh?*) 비가 올 것 같지요?

It's awfully hot, isn't it!
Mopshi topkunyo! (*Mope-she tup-kuun-yoh!*) 몹시덥군요!

It's raining!
Pi ga wayo! (*Pee gah wah-yoh!*) 비가 와요!

It's very windy.
Parami mani puroyo. (*Pah-rah-me mah-nee puu-ruh-yoh*) 바람이 많이 불어요.

Do you think it will rain tomorrow?
Naeil pi ga ogessumnikka? (*Nay-eel pee gah ah-gay-sume-nee-kah?*) 내일 비가 오겠습니까?

No, it will not rain tomorrow.
Anio, naeilen pi ga ahn ol kot katayo.
(*Ah'-n yoh naeilen pi ga ahn ol kot katohl kaht kah-ta-yoh*) 아니오, 내일은 비가 안 올 것 같아요.

It's snowing!
Nun-i wayo! (*Nuun-ee wah-yoh!*) 눈이 와요!

What is the forecast for tomorrow?
Naeil ilgi yebonun? *(Nay-eel eel-ghee yeh-buh-nuun?)*
내일 일기 예보는?

* Please keep in mind that the hyphenated Romanized phonetics (e.g. *Nay-eel*) should be pronounced in a smooth, even flow. Read them out loud several times to train your tongue and lips in making the proper sounds smoothly.

52 Mood *Kibun* *(Kee-boon)* 기분

bored	*simsimhaeyo* *(sheem-sheem-hay-yoh)* 심심해요
frustrated	*dapdaphaeyo* *(dahp-dahp-hay-yoh)* 답답해요
interested	*jaemi issoyo* *(jay-mee-ee-suh-yoh)* 재미있어요
disinterested	*jaemi opoyo* *(jay-mee-ope-suh-yoh)* 재미없어요
in a good mood	*kibuni choayo* *(kee-boon-ee choh-ah-yoh)* 기분이 좋아요
in a bad mood	*kibuni napayo* *(kee-boon-ee nah-pah-yoh)* 기분이 나빠요

I am bored.
Chunun simsimhaeyo. *(Chuh-nuun sheem-sheem-hay-yoh)*
저는 심심해요.

The movie was fun.
Yonghwaga jaemi issosoyo. *(Yuhng-hwah-gah jay-mee-ee-suh-suh-yoh)* 영화가 재미있었어요.

It is fun learning Korean.
Hangug orul paeunun gosun jaemi issoyo. *(Hahn-guug oh-ruhl pay-uu-nuun guh-suun jay-mee-ee-suh-yoh)*
한국어를 배우는 것은 재미있어요.

How do you feel today?
Onul kibuni otteyo? *(Oh-nuhl kee-boon-ee ah-ttay-yoh?)*
오늘 기분이 어때요?

I am in a good mood.
Kibuni choayo. *(Kee-boon-ee choh-ah-yoh)*
기분이 좋아요.

I am ok.
Goenchanayo. *(Goehn-chahn-ah-yoh)* 괜찮아요.

53 Personality *Songyok* *(Sahng-yoke)* 성격

good	*chakhaeyo* *(chack-hay-yoh)* 착해요
smart	*ttokttokhaeyo* *(toke-toke-hay-yoh)* 똑똑해요
dumb	*mungchunghaeyo* *(muhng-chuhng-hay-yoh)* 멍청해요
meticulous	*komkomhaeyo* *(kohm-kohm-hay-yoh)* 꼼꼼해요
friendly	*chinjolhaeyo* *(cheen-juhl-hay-yoh)* 친절해요
unfriendly	*bulchinjolhaeyo* *(buhl-cheen-juhl-hay-yoh)* 불친절해요
selfish	*igijeok ieyo* *(ee-geeh-joak-ee-eh-yoh)* 이기적이에요
stubborn	*kochipi seyo* *(koh-cheep-ee se-yoh)* 고집이 세요

humble	*kyomsonhaeyo (k'yohm-sohn-hay-yoh)* 겸손해요
act like one is so great	*chalran chokhaeyo (chahl-rahn choak-hay-yoh)* 잘난 척해요
be awkward	*sumoksumokhaeyo (suh-muhk-suh-muhk-hay-yoh)* 서먹서먹 해요
be good friends with	*chinhaeyo (cheen-hay-yoh)* 친해요
get along well with	*saiga choayo (sah-ee-gah-choh-ah-yoh)* 사이가 좋아요
have good social skills	*sakyosunge choayo (sah-k'yoh-suhng-ee choh-ah-yoh)* 사교성이 좋아요

You are very kind!
Chungmal chinjolhasineyo! (Chung-mahl cheen-juhl-ha-she-nay-yoh!) 정말 친절하시네요!

Are you a good friend of his/hers? (OR **Are you his/her good friend?**)
Ku saram hago chinhaseyo? (Kuu sah-rahm-hah-goh cheen-hah-say-yoh?) 그 사람하고 친하세요?

I am not close to him/her.
Chunun ku saram hago sumoksumokhaeyo.
(Chuh-nuun kuu sah-rahm-hah-goh suh-muhk-suh-muhk-hay-yoh) 저는 그 사람하고 서먹서먹 해요.

What is he/she like?
Ku saram otteyo? (Kuu sah-rahm ah-ttay-yoh?)
그 사람 어때요?

We get along well with each other.
Urinun saiga choayo. (Uu-ree-nuun sah-ee-gah-choh-ah-yoh) 우리는 사이가 좋아요.

Are you his good friend?
Ku saram hago chinhaseyo?

What is he like?
Ku saram otteyo?

I am not close to him.
Chunun ku saram hago sumoksumokhaeyo.

Do You Know me?

Handsome.
Chal sang-kyoutsoyo.

Cool.
Mushissoyo.

I Love Me!

And act like he is so great!
Chalran chokhaeyo!

Appearance *Oemo* (Whay-moh) 외모

pretty	**yepuyo** (yeh-puh-yoh) 예뻐요
handsome	**chal sangkyoutsoyo** (chal-sang-k'yoht-suh-yoh) 잘 생겼어요
ugly	**mot sangkyoutsoyo** (mote-sang-k'yoht-suh-yoh) 못 생겼어요
cute	**gwiyowoyo** (gwee-yuh-woh-yoh) 귀여워요
cool	**mushissoyo** (mu-shee-ssuh-yoh) 멋있어요
slim	**nalshinhaeyo** (nahl-sheen-hay-yoh) 날씬해요
fat	**tungtunghaeyo** (tuhng-tuhng-hay-yoh) 뚱뚱해요
pale	**changpaekhaeyo** (chahng-pake-hay-yoh) 창백해요
gain weight	**sari jot ssoyo** (sah-ree jot-suh-yoh) 살이 쪘어요
lost weight	**sari bbajo ssoyo** (sah-ree bbah-juh-suh-yoh) 살이 빠졌어요
go on a diet	**dietrul haeyo** (diet-ruhl hay-yoh) 다이어트를 해요

Talking about one's physical appearance
It is not common, and sometimes rude, to talk about physical appearance, e.g. someone being "fat" or "slim," but in Korea you will hear the words used quite often across gender and age. This interest in physical appearance covers many physical attributes—such as noses, eyes, height, and size of faces.

What does he/she look like?
Ku sarameun ottoke sangkyoutsoyo?
(Kuu sah-rahm-unn aht-tah-keh sang-k'yoht-suh-yoh)
그 사람은 어떻게 생겼어요?

He is handsome.
Ku sarameun chal sangkyoutsoyo.
(Kuu sah-rahm-unn chal-sang-k'yoht-suh-yoh)
그 사람은 잘 생겼어요.

Your puppy is cute.
Kangajiga gwiyowoyo.
(Kahng-ah-jee-gah gwee-yuh-woh-yoh)
강아지가 귀여워요.

You look pale, are you ok?
Changpaekhae boinun de, goenchanayo? *(Chahng-pake-hay boh-ee-nuun day, goehn-chahn-ah-yoh?)* 창백해 보이는데, 괜찮아요?

I gain weight these days.
Yojum sari jot ssoyo. *(Yoh-juhm sah-ree jot-suh-yoh)*
요즘 살이 쪘어요.

---

55 Airline / Airport *Hanggong hoesa* *(Hahng-gong hway-sah)* 항공 회사 / *Konghang* *(Kong-hahng)* 공항

airline terminal 1	*che-il chongsa* *(chuh-eel chohng-sah)* 제 일 청사
airline terminal 2	*che-i chongsa* *(chuh-ee chohng-sah)* 제 이 청사
domestic terminal	*kungnae chongsa* *(kuung-nay chohng-sah)* 국내 청사
airplane	*pi-hang-gi* *(pee-hang-ghee)* 비행기

international flight	**kukjeson** (kuuk-jay-sahn) 국제선
domestic flight	**kuknaeson** (kuuk-nay-sahn) 국내선
non-stop flight	**jighang** (jeeg-hahng) 직항
lay over	**kyongyu** (k'yohng-yuu) 경유
transfer	**hwan sung** (hwahn- suhng) 환승
boarding	**tapsung** (tahp-suung) 탑승
boarding gate	**tapsungu** (tahp-suung-guu) 탑승구
check-in	**tapsung susok** (tahp-suung suu-soak) 탑승 수속
first class	**il-dung sok** (eel-duhng suhk) 일등석
business class	**businesssok** (business-suhk) 비지니스석
economy class	**ilbansok** (eel-bahn suhk) 일반석
seat	**chwa sok** (chwah soak) 좌석
arrival	**ipgu** (eep-guu) 입국
departure	**chulguk** (chuul-guuk) 출국
plane captain	**kijang** (kee-jahng) 기장
flight attendant	**sungmuwon** (suhg-muu-won) 승무원
passenger	**sunggaek** (suhng-gake) 승객
duty-free shop	**myon-se jom** (m'yone-say-juhm) 면세점

How do I get to the airport?
Konghang-e ottoke gayo? (Kong-hahng-eh aht-tah-keh gah-yoh?) 공항에 어떻게 가요?

What time do I have to check in?
Myoshie chekuin-rul haeya dwaeyo? (Mwuh-she-eh check-in-ruhl hay-yah dway-yoh?) 몇 시에 체크인을 해야 돼요?

Where do I check-in?
Tapsung susok hanun tega odieyo?
(Tahp-suung suu-soak hah-nuun deh-ga ah-dee-eh-yoh?)
탑승 수속 하는 데가 어디예요?

Where is the departure gate?
Chulbalhanun tega odieyo? *(Chuhl-bahl-hah-nuun deh-ga ah-dee-eh-yoh?)* 출발하는 데가 어디예요?

Churgukjange odieyo? *(Chuul-guuk-jahng-ee ah-dee-eh-yoh?)* 출국장이 어디예요?

I want to change my seat.
Chwa sok ul pakugo shipundeyo. *(Chwah-soak-uhl pahku-goh ship-uhn-deh-yoh)* 좌석을 바꾸고 싶은데요.

Where is the baggage claim?
Chim chatnun tega odieyo? *(Cheem chat-nuun deh-ga ah-dee-eh-yoh?)* 짐 찾는 데가 어디예요?

I lost my baggage.
Chimul ilruborutssoyo. *(Cheem-uhl ee-ruh-buh-rut-soh-yoh)* 짐을 잃어버렸어요.

How long does it take to fly to Chejudo Island?
Chejudo kaji olmana kollyo yo? *(Jeh-juu-do kah-jee ohl-mah-nah kohl-lay-oh-yoh?)* 제주도까지 얼마나 걸려요?

What time does the duty free shop open?
Myon-se jome myoshie yoloyo? *(M'yone-say-juhm-ee mwuh-she-eh yuhl-uh-yoh?)* 면세점이 몇시에 열어요?

Where can I change money?
Ton-eul odiso hwanjun haeyo? *(Tone-yule ah-dee-soh wahn-juhn-hay-yoh?)* 돈을 어디서 환전해요?

Where is the bus stop to downtown?
Toshimji-ro kanun bosu chongnyujange odi issumnika?
(*Toh-sheem-jee-roh kah-nuun buh-suu chong-n'yuu-jahng-ee ah-dee e-sume-nee-kah?*)
도심지로 가는 버스 정류장이 어디 있습니까?

Where is a subway station?
Chihachol yok-i odiso yo? (*Jee-hah-chuhl yuhk-ee ah-dee-suh yoh?*) 지하철 역이 어딨어요?

Taxi(s) *Taekshi* (*Tack-she*) 택시

Where can I catch a taxi?
Taekshi odiso chapchiyo? (*Tahk-she ah-dee-soh chahp-chee-yoh?*) 택시 어디서 잡지요?

Please call a taxi for me.
Taekshi-rul pullo chuseyo. (*Tahk-she-ruhl puhl-yoh chuu-say-oh*) 택시를 불러주세요.

Please take me to the airport.
Ja-rul gong-hang-e diryada juseyo.
(*Jah-ruhl gohng-hahng-eh dee-r'yaw-dah juu-say-yoh*)
저를 공항에 데려다 주세요.

How much does it cost to go to the airport by taxi?
Konghang-kka-ji taekshi yogom-i eolmayeyo?
(*Koong-hahng-kkah-jee tahk-she yoh-guum-ee eh-yohl-mah-yay-yoh?*) 공항까지 택시요금이 얼마에요?

Please take me to the _____ hotel.
_____ ho'tel kkaji kapshida. (*_____ hotel kkah-jee kahp-she-dah*) _____ 호텔까지 갑시다.

Take me to this address.
I chusoro chomka chuseyo. (Ee chuu-soh-roh chome-kah chuu-say-yoh) 이 주소로 좀 가주세요.

Please wait for me.
Yogi-seo kidaryo chushigesseoyo.
(Yoh-ghee seh-oh kee-dah-rio chuu-she-gay-say-oh-yoh)
여기서 기다려 주시겠어요.

Please take me downtown.
Shinae chom ka chuseyo. (She-nay chome kah chuu-say-yoh) 시내 좀 가주세요.

How much (is the taxi fare)?
Eol mayeyo? (Eh-ohl mah-yay-oh?) 얼마예요?

* Regular taxis in Korea routinely pick up additional passengers who are going in the same general direction as their first passenger, in order to boost their income—a custom known as *hapsung (hop-suung)*. The practice is illegal but widely carried out. People wanting a taxi shout out their destinations to drivers, who slow down when they see potential passengers waving at them. *Hapsung* is especially common during bad weather.

here   *yogi (yuh-ghee)* 여기

Please stop here.
Yogi-seo sewo chuseyo. (Yuh-ghee-suh-oh say-woh chuu-say-yoh) 여기서 세워 주세요.

Please wait here.
Yogiso kidarishipshio. (Yuh-ghee-suh kee-dah-ree-ship-she-oh) 여기서 기다리십시요.

hurry   *soduruda (suh-duu-ruh-dah)* 서두르다

I'm in a hurry.
Cho-nun soduru-go issumnida (Choh-nuun suh-duh-ruh-go e-sume-nee-dah) 저는 서두르고 있습니다.

there   *kogi (kuh-ghee)* 거기

Please put the bag there.
Kabangul kogie noushio.
(Kah-bahng-uhl kuh-ghee-eh no-uh-she-oh)
가방을 거기에 놓으시오.

left   *wentchogui (went-johg-we)* 왼쪽의

Turn left at the next corner.
Taum motungieso wentchoguro toshio. (Tah-uum moh-tuung-ee-ee-suh went-johg-uu-roh toh-she-oh) 다음 모퉁이
에서 왼쪽으로 도시오.

right   *oruntchogui (oh-ruhnt-johg-we)* 오른쪽의
straight   *ttokparun (toke-pah-ruhn)* 똑바른

Turn at the next corner.
Taum motung-i eso toseyo. (Tah-uum moh-tuung-ee eh-suh toh-say-yoh) 다음 모퉁이에서 도세요.

57 Subway *Chihachol* *(Jee-hah-chuhl)* 지하철

Subway lines in Korea are color-coded, with platform signs in Korean, English and Chinese characters. Many major stations are virtual art galleries, with public areas for people to meet friends, rest, read, etc.

subway station	***chihachol yok*** (*jee-hah-chuhl yuhk*) 지하철역
ticket	***pyo*** (*p'-yoh*) 표
ticket machine	***chapyo chadong panmaegi*** (*chahp-yoh chah-dohng pahn-may-ghee*) 차표 자동 판매기
ticket office	***maepyo so*** (*mape-yoh soh*) 매표소
ticket window	***maepyo gu*** (*mape-yoh-guu*) 매표구

Where is a subway station?

Chihachol yok-i odiso yo? (*Jee-hah-chuhl yuhk-ee ah-dee-suh yoh?*) 지하철 역이 어딨어요?

Do you have a subway map in English?

Yong-o-ro toen chihachol chidoga isseoyo? (*Yuhng-oh roh toh-un chee-hah-chohl chee-doh-gah ees-say-oh-yoh?*) 영어로 된 지하철 지도가 있어요?

Where should I get off to go to _____?

_____ ***e-karyo myon odiso naeryeo-ya twaeyo?*** (_____ *eh-kah-rio m'yohn ah-dee-sah nay-ray-oh-yah tway-yoh?*) _____ 에 가려면 어디서 내려야 돼요?

Where should I get off to transfer to Line No. 2?

Ihosun kalah taryo myon odiso naeryeo-ya twaeyo? (*Ee-ho-sun-eu-ro khal-ah-tah-rio m'yohn ah-dee-sah nay-ray-oh-yah tway-yoh?*) 2호선으로 갈아타려면 어디서 내려야 해요?

How much is the fare?

Yogum un olmaimnikka? (*Yoh-guum uhn ohl-my-mm-nee-kah?*) 요금은 얼마입니까?

Where can I buy a ticket?
P'yo odiso salsu issoyo? (P'yoh ah-dee-sah sahl-suu ee-sah-yoh?) 표 어디서 살 수 있어요?

Bus *Bosu* (Buh-suu) 버스

1st class metro bus	*chwa sok bosu (chwah soak buh-suu)* 좌석버스
regular metro bus	*shinae bosu (she-nay buh-suu)* 시내버스
inter-city bus	*kan-sun bosu (kang-suu buh-suu)* 간선버스
town, village bus	*chikaeng bosu (jee-kang buh-suu)* 직행버스
neighborhood bus	*maul bosu (mah-uhl buh-suu)* 마을버스
bus stop	*bosu jongryujang (buh-suu johng-rue-jahng)* 버스 정류장
express bus	*kosok bosu (koh-soak buh-suu)* 고속버스
sightseeing bus	*kwangwang bosu (kwahng-gwahng buh-suu)* 관광버스
prepaid electronic transit pass	*kyotong kadu (k'yoh-tong kah-duu)* 교통카드

How much is the fare?
Yogum un olma jiyo? (Yoh-guum uhn ohl-mah jee-yoh?) 요금은 얼마지요?

Is there a bus stop near here?
I kuchoe bosu chongnyujangi issumnikka? (Ee kuu-choh-eh buh-suu chohng-nyuu-jahn-ghee e-sume-nee-kah?) 이 근처에 버스 정류장이 있습니까?

Is there a bus to downtown?
Toshimji-ro kanun bosu pyoni issumnika? (Toh-sheem-jee-roh kah-nuun buh-suu p'yoh-nee e-sume-nee-kah?)
도심지로 가는 버스편이 있습니까?

How often do buses run?
Bosu ga myoppunmada wayo? (Buh-suu gah m'yahp-puun-mah-dah wah-yoh?) 버스가 몇 분마다 와요?

Which bus goes to _____?
Myoppon bosu ga _____ e kayo? (M'yahp-puun buh-suu ga _____ eh kah-yoh?) 몇 번 버스가____ 에 가요?

Does this bus go to _____?
I bosu ga _____ e kayo? (Ee buh-suu ga _____ eh kah-yoh?) 이 버스가 _____ 에 가요?

Please let me off here.
Naeryo juseyo. (Nay-rio juu-say-yoh) 내려주세요.

Where can I buy a bus card?
Kyotong kadurul odiso sayo? (K'yoh-tong kah-duu-ruhl ah-dee-suh sah-yoh?) 교통카드를 어디서 사요?

Where can I recharge a bus card?
Kyotong kadurul odiso chungjunhaeyo?
(K'yoh-tong kah-duu-ruhl ah-dee-suh chung-juhn hay-yoh?)
교통카드를 어디서 충전해요?

---

59 ## Cars *Jadongcha* (Jah-dong-chah) 자동차

driver	*unjonsu (uun-chone-suu)* 운전수	
driver's license	*unjon myonhojung (uun-juhn m'yuhn-huh-juung)* 운전면허증	
parking lot	*jucha jang (juu-chah jahng)* 주차장	

no parking	*jucha jeumji* (*juu-chah jome-jee*) 주차 금지
service station	*jadongcha juyuso* (*jah-dong-chah juu-yuu-sah*) 자동차 주유소
speed limit	*sokto jehan* (*soak-toh jay-hahn*) 속도 제한
insurance	*pohom* (*poh-home*) 보험

I would like to rent a car.
Cha-rul piligo shipsseumnida. (*Chah-ruhl pee-lee-go ship-sume-nee-dah*) 차를 빌리고 싶습니다.

Where can I rent a car?
Odiso cha rentu halsu issoyo? (*Ah-dee-sah chah ren-tuu hahl-suu ee-sah-yoh?*) 어디서 차 렌트 할 수 있어요?

I also need a driver.
Yokshi unjonsuga piryo hamnida. (*Yuk-she uun-john-suu ga pee-rio hahm-nee-dah*) 역시 운전수가 필요합니다.

How much (is the rental) by the day?
Harue olmaeyo? (*Hah-ruu-eh uhl-may-yoh?*) 하루에 얼마예요?

Where is the gas station?
Juyusoga odie issoyo? (*Juu-yuu-sah-gah ah-dee-eh ee-sah-yoh?*) 주유소가 어디에 있어요?

60 Trains *Kicha* (*Kee-chah*) 기차

| express train | *saemaul-ho* (*say-mahl-hoh*) 새마을호 |
| semi-express | *mugunghwa-ho* (*muu-guung-hwah-hoh*) 무궁화호 |

local stops	*tong-il-ho* (*tohng-eel-hoh*) 통일호
conductor	*chajang* (*chah-jahng*) 차장
one-way ticket	*pyondo pyo* (*p'yohn-doh*) 편도표
round-trip ticket	*wanbok pyo* (*wahn-boak p'yoh*) 왕복표
student ticket	*haksang pyo* (*hahk-sang p'yoh*) 학생표
senior citizen's ticket	*noin/kyongno pyo* (*noh-een k'yohng p'yoh*) 노인/경노표
first-class seat	*il-dung sok* (*eel-duung-suk*) 일등석
second-class seat	*i-dung sok* (*ee-duung suk*) 이등석
standing room ticket	*ip sok* (*eep suk*) 입석
dining car	*shiktang cha* (*sheek-tahng chah*) 식당차

Is this the train for Pusan?
Pusan hang yol cha-e yoh?
(*Buu-sahn hang yohl chah-eh yoh?*) 부산행 열차예요?

Two tickets to Pusan, please.
Pusan hang kicha pyo-rul tu chang chuseyo. (*Buu-sahn hang kee-chah p'yoh-ruhl tuu chahng chuu-say-yoh*)
부산행 기차표를 두 장 주세요.

What number is the dining car?
Shiktang cha-nun myopon imnikka? (*Sheek-tahng chah-nuun myah-puhn eem-nee-kkah?*) 식당차는 몇 번입니까?

sleeping car	*chimdae cha* (*cheem-day chah*) 침대차

What number is the sleeping car?
Chimdae cha-nun myoppon imnikka? (*Cheem-day chah-nuun m'yahp-puhn eem-nee-kkah?*) 침대차는 몇번 입니까?

What station is this?
Yogi-ga musun yogie yo? (*Yuu-ghee-gah muu-suhn yuu-ghee-eh yoh?*) 여기가 무슨 역이에요?

Which is the next station?
Taum yogi odie yo? (*Tah-uum yu-ghee ah-dee-eh yoh?*) 다음 역이 어디에요?

I want to get off at Taegu.
Taegu eso naeriryogo hanun deyo. (*Tay-guu eh-suh nay-ree-r'yoh-go hah-nuun day-yoh*) 대구에서 내리려고 하는데요.

Bathroom / Toilet
Hwajangshil (*Hwah-jahang-sheel*) 화장실

American-style bathroom/ restroom	*yokshil* (*yoke-sheel*) 욕실/ *hwajanshil* (*hwah-jahang-sheel*) 화장실
toilet paper	*hyuji* (*hugh-jee*) 휴지
public bathhouse	*mokyok tang* (*moke-yoke-tahng*) 목욕탕
sink	*semyonde* (*seh-m'yohn-day*) 세면대
bath tub	*yokjo* (*yoke-joh*) 욕조
soap	*pinu* (*pee-nuu*) 비누
mirror	*keoul* (*kuh-uhl*) 거울
toothbrush	*chitsol* (*chee-sohl*) 칫솔
toothpaste	*chiyak* (*chee-yak*) 치약
towel	*sukun* (*suu-kuhn*) 수건

Where is a/the restroom?
Hwajang-shil-i odi issoyo? (*Hwah-jahng sheel-ee ah-dee-saw?*) 화장실이 어디 있어요?

Hotels *Hot'el* (*Hoh-tel*) 호텔

guesthouse	*minbakchip* (*meen-bahk-cheep*) 민박집
motel	*motel / yogwan* (*yuh-gwahn*) 모텔
family-run bed-and-breakfast type facilities	*minbak* (*meen-bahk*) 민박
reservations	*yeyak* (*yay-yahk*) 예약
to confirm	*hwaginhada* (*hwah-geen-hah-dah*) 확인하다

room	***pang*** (*pahng*) 방
room charge	***pang kap*** (*pahng kahp*) 방값
room number	***pang ponho*** (*pahng bahn-hoh*) 방번호
room key	***pang yolsweo*** (*pahng yahl-swah*) 방열쇠
single bed	***ilinyong chimdae*** (*eel-een-yong cheem-day*) 일인용 침대
double bed	***iinyong chimdae*** (*e-een-yong cheem-day*) 이인용 침대
front desk	***chop sugyee*** (*chup suu-geh-eh*) 접수계
bath	***mogyok tang*** (*moag-yoke tahng*) 목욕탕
shower	***swawoe*** (*sha-wah*) 샤워
inn (Korean)	***yogwan*** (*yuh-gwahn*) 여관
hotel taxi	***hotel taekshi*** (*hoh-tel tack-she*) 호텔 택시

I made a reservation.
Yeyak hattnundeyo. (*Yay-yahk hatt-nunn-day-yoh*)
예약 했는데요.

Can I pay with a credit card?
Kureditu kadu-ro kyesan dwae yo?
(*Kuu-ray-dee-tuu kah-duu- roh keh-sahn dway yoh?*)
크레디트 카드로 계산 돼요?

Do you take travelers' checks?
Yohaeng-ja supyo pada yo? (*Yuh-hang-jah suup-yoh pah-dah yoh?*) 여행자 수표 받아요?

What time do I have to check out?
Myoshie chekuout-sul haeya dwaeyo?
(Mwuh-she-eh check-out-suhl hay-yah dway-yoh?)
몇 시에 체크아웃을 해야 돼요?

Can you give me a wake up call?
Morning call dwaeyo? *(Morning-call dway-yoh?)*
모닝콜 돼요?

Can I order room service?
Rum sobisu dwae yo? *(Rume sah-bee-suu dway yoh?)*
룸서비스 돼요?

Is there a safe in the room?
Bange kumgoga issuyo? *(Bahng-eh kuum-go-gah ee-sah-yoh?)* 방에 금고가 있어요?

63 | Eating *Mokta* *(Muhk-tah)* 먹다

dining	*siksa* *(sheek-sah)* 식사	
breakfast	*achim* *(ah-cheem)* 아침	
lunch	*chomshim* *(chume-sheem)* 점심	
dinner	*chonyok* *(chune-yuuk)* 저녁	
side dishes	*pan chan* *(pahn chahn)* 반찬	
menu	*menyu* *(meh-nyuu)* 메뉴	
snack	*kansik* *(kahn-sheek)* 간식	
dessert	*husik* *(huu-sheek)* 후식/*tijotu* *(dee-jah-tuu)* 디저트	
fork	*poku* *(poh-kuu / foh-kuu)* 포크	
knife	*naipu* *(nie-puh / nie-fuu)* 나이프	
spoon	*sukkarak* *(suuk-kah-rahk)* 숟가락	
chopsticks	*chokkarak* *(chuuk-kah-rahk)* 젓가락	
toothpick	*issushigae* *(ee-suu-she-gay)* 이쑤시개	
food	*umshik* *(uhm-sheek)* 음식	

Korean food	*Hanguk umshik* (*Hahn-guuk uhm-sheek*) 한국 음식 / *Hanshik* (*Hahn-sheek*) 한식
Chinese food	*Chungguk umshik* (*Chuung-guuk uhm-sheek*) 중국 음식 / *Chungshik* (*Chuung-sheek*) 중식
Western food	*Soyang umshik* (*Sah-yahng uhm-sheek*) 서양 음식 / *Yangshik* (*Yahng-sheek*) 양식
Japanese food	*Ilbon umshik* (*Eel-bone uhm-sheek*) 일본 음식 / *Ilshik* (*Eel-sheek*) 일식
bread	*pang* (*pahng*) 빵
rice (cooked)	*pap* (*pahp*) 밥
beef	*sokogi* (*so-koh-ghee*) 소고기
chicken	*takkogi* (*tahk-koh-ghee*) 닭고기
eggs	*talgyal* (*tahl-g'yahl*) 달걀/ *kyeran* (*kay-rahn*) 계란
squid	*ojingah* (*oh-jeeng-ah*) 오징어
noodles	*kuksu* (*kuuk-suh*) 국수
seaweed	*kim* (*keem*) 김
tofu	*tu-bu* (*tuh-buhh*) 두부
fish	*saengson* (*sang-suhn*) 생선
broiled fish	*saengson gui* (*sang-sahn gway*) 생선 구이
pork	*twaejigogi* (*tway-jee-go-ghee*) 돼지구이
pork ribs	*twaejigal bi* (*tway-jee-gahl bee*) 돼지 갈비
beef ribs	*gal-bi* (*gahl-bee*) 갈비
roast beef	*pulgogi* (*buhl-go-ghee*) 불고기
noodles with meat and vegetables	*chap chae* (*chop-chay*) 잡채

green onion pancake	**pachon** *(pah-chune)* 파전
beef rib soup	**galbitang** *(gahl-bee-thang)* 갈비탕
soy bean paste stew	**doenjangjjigae** *(doen-jang-jji-gae)* 된장찌개
kimchi stew	**kimchijjigae** *(kim-chee-jji-gae)* 김치찌개
soup	**kuk** *(kuuk)* 국
cold chewy noodles	**naengmyun** *(naeng-m'yohn)* 냉면
rice mixed with vegetable	**bibimpap** *(bi-bim-pahp)* 비빔밥
skewered beef and vegetables	**san jeok** *(sahn joak)* 산적

* When you go to a Korean restaurant, you will inevitably see the following terms associated with food.

-볶음 **pokum** *(poak-uhm)* ⎫
-볶기 **pokki** *(poak-kee)* ⎬ lightly stir-fried dish
-볶이 **pokki** *(poak-kee)* ⎭
-찌개 **jjigae** *(jee-gay)* salty stew
-탕 **tang** *(tahng)* soup based on meat broth
-구이 **gui** *(gway)* broiled meat or fish
-면 **myon** *(m'yone)* noodles
-전 **chon** *(chune)* thin, savory Korean pancakes
-밥 **pap** *(pahp)* rice-based dish
불- **bul** *(bhul)* broiled or barbecued over open fire

vegetables	*yachae* (*yah-chay*) 야채
cabbage	*yangbaechu* (*yahng-bae-chuu*) 양배추
onion	*yangpa* (*yahng-pah*) 양파
carrot	*dangun* (*dang-guhn*) 당근
potato	*kamja* (*kahm-jah*) 감자
sweet potato	*kokuma* (*ko-kuu-mah*) 고구마
cucumber	*oi* (*oh-ee*) 오이
squash	*hobak* (*hoh-bahk*) 호박
mushroom	*bosot* (*buh-sut*) 버섯
spinach	*shikumchi* (*shee-kuhm-chee*) 시금치
bean sprouts	*kongnamul* (*kong-nah-muhl*) 콩나물

seasoning	*yangnyom* (*yahng-n'yohm*) 양념
salt	*sogum* (*soh-guhm*) 소금
pepper	*huchu* (*huu-chu*) 후추
sugar	*soltang* (*sohl-tahng*) 설탕
soy sauce	*kanjang* (*kahn-jahng*) 간장
vinegar	*shikcho* (*sheek-choh*) 식초
red pepper powder	*kochutgaru* (*ko-chuut-gah-ruu*) 고춧가루
red pepper paste	*kochujang* (*ko-chuu-jahng*) 고추장

fruit	*kwail* (*kwah-eel*) 과일
apple	*sagwa* (*sahg-wah*) 사과
pear	*pae* (*pay*) 배
grapes	*podo* (*poh-doh*) 포도
watermelon	*subak* (*suu-bahk*) 수박
strawberry	*ddalki* (*ddahl-kee*) 딸기
tangerine	*kyull* (*kyuhll*) 귤

taste	*mat (mhat)* 맛
tasty	*madissoyo (mah-dee-suh-yoh)* 맛있어요
not tasty	*matupssoyo (mah-dup-suh-yoh)* 맛없어요
spicy	*maewoyo (may-woh-yoh)* 매워요
salty	*jayo (jah-yoh)* 짜요
bitter	*ssoyo (ssuh-yoh)* 써요
sour	*shoyo (shah-yoh)* 셔요
hot*	*ddugowoyo (dduu-gah-wah-yoh)* 뜨거워요
cold*	*chagawoyo (chah-gah-wah-yoh)* 차가워요
bland	*singguwoyo (shing-guh-woh-yoh)* 싱거워요
sweet	*dalayo (dahl-ah-yoh)* 달아요

* The two words associated with heat —"hot" *dugowoyo (duu-gah-wah-yoh)* 뜨거워요 and "cold" *chagawoyo (chah-gah-wah yoh)* 차가워요—are only used when describing the temperature of physical things. For describing the weather or air temperature, use *towoyo (tah-wah-yoh)* 더워요 for "hot," and *chuwoyo (chuu-wah-yoh)* 추워요 for "cold."

In a Korean restaurant

I'm hungry.
Chonun paego p'ayo. (Chuh-nuun pay-goh pah-yoh)
저는 배 고파요.

I'm full.
Chonun pae pulroyo. (Chuh-nuun pay-puul-ruh-yoh)
저는 배 불러요.

What kind of food do you like?
Musun eumsicul choahaseyo? (*Muh-sun eum-shic-ul choh-ah-hah-say-yoh?*) 무슨 음식을 좋아하세요?

What would you like to eat?
Mwo mokko shipuseyo?
(*Mwah mokko ship-eu-say-yoh?*) 뭐 먹고 싶으세요?

I would like to eat Chinese food.
Chungguk-umshik-rul mokko shipundeyo.
(*Chuung-guuk- uhm-sheek-ruhl moke-koh ship-uhn-deh-yoh*)
중국음식을 먹고 싶은데요.

Do you have a menu in English?
Yong-o-ro doen menu issoyo?
(*Yung-uu-roh doh-en men-yuu ee-suh-yoh?*)
영어로 된 메뉴 있어요?

Please start (eating).
Deuseyo. (*Deu-say-yoh*) 드세요.

Thank you for the food.
*Chal mokke ssumnida.** (*Chahl moke-kuh sume-nee-dah*)
잘 먹겠습니다.

* Literally, I will eat well.

I have enjoyed the food.
*Chal mogossupnida.** (*Chahl moh-guh-suhm-ni-dah*)
잘 먹었습니다.

* Literally, I ate well.

Just a little, please.
Choguman, juseyo. (*Choh-guhm-mhan, juu-say-yoh*)
조금만 주세요.

Is this dish spicy?
I umshig maewoyo? (*Ee uhm-sheeg may-woh-yoh?*)
이 음식 매워요?

I cannot eat spicy food.
Chonun maewon umshikul mot mokauyo.
(*Chuh-nunn may-won uhm-sheek-uhl mot mok-ah-yoh*)
저는 매운 음식을 못 먹어요.

I am allergic to cucumber.
Chonun oi allerugiga issuyo. (*Chuh-nuun oh-ee ahl-ehh-ruh-ghee-gah issu-yoh*) 저는 오이 알레르기가 있어요.

I will give you a treat → I will pay.
Chega sa ket ssumnida. (*Cheh-gah sah-keht sume-nee-dah*)
제가 사겠습니다.

Then, I will pay for a dessert.
Gurom chega hushikul sa ket ssumnida.
(*Guu-rahm cheh-gah huu-sheek-uhl sah-keht sume-nee-dah*)
그럼 제가 후식을 사겠습니다.

What would you like to order?
Chumun hashi ge sseo yo? (*Chu-munn-ha-she-guh-soh-yoh?*) 주문하시겠어요?

I will have _____please.
Chonun _____ juseyo. (*Chuh-nuun _____ juu-say-yoh*) 저는 _____ 주세요.

Calling a waiter or waitress
In a Korean restaurant, a waiter/waitress rarely checks on you unless you call them. It is considered rude to speak to a customer who is eating. If you meet a waiter or waitress who is significantly older than you, address the older

waitress *ajumoni* (*ah-juu-moh-nee*) 아주머니 (meaning "aunt"), and an older waiter *ajossi* (*ah-juh-she*) 아저씨 (meaning "uncle"). A typical Korean restaurant hires more waitresses than waiters. Since it is not always easy to figure out everyone's respective ages, customers would just call out "here" 여기요 *yogiyoh* (*yoh-ghee-yoh*) or "there" 저기요 *chogiyo* (*choh-ghee-yoh*) to get the attention of the waiter / waitress.

Excuse me, please bring me a fork.
Ajumoni, poku-rul katta chushipshio. (*Ah-juu-moh-nee, poh-kuu-ruhl kaht-tah chuu-ship-she-oh*) 아주머니 포크를 갖다주십시요.

Excuse me, (Bring me some) bread, please.
Yogiyoh, pang chom chuseyo. (*Yoh-ghee-yoh, pahng chome chuu-say-yoh*) 여기요, 빵 좀 주세요.

Asking for more side dishes
In a Korean restaurant, at least three or more side dishes will be served before the main dish. These are served as part of the service; the customer does not need to ask for them. It is very common to ask for more side dishes when the first ones are consumed, and you are not charged for the additional ones.

Excuse me, give me more side dishes, please.
Yogiyoh pan chan chom to juseyo. (*yoh-ghee-yoh pahn-chahn chome tah juu-say-yoh*) 여기요 반찬 좀 더 주세요.

---

64 Drinks *Umnyo* (*Uhm-n'yoh*) 음료

| to drink | *mashida* (*mah-she-dah*) 마시다 |
| alcoholic drink | *sul* (*suhl*) 술 |

89

bar (for drinking)   *ppa (bah)* 바
bar snacks   *anju (ahn-juu)** 안주

* Some bars require that patrons automatically accept side dishes of *anju* as a kind of cover charge.

karaoke place   *norae bang (no-ray bahng)* 노래방
    (literally, "song room")

I'm thirsty.
Chonun mogmallayo. (Chuh-nuun mog-mahl-lah-yoh)
저는 목 말라요.

What are you doing this evening?
Onulbame mwo haseyo? (Oh-nuhl-bah-meh mwah hah-say-yoh?) 오늘밤에 뭐하세요?

Let's have a drink.
Muot jom mashipshida. (Mwaht johm mah-ship-she-dah)
뭣 좀 마십시다.

I don't drink alcohol.
Chunun sul mothamnida.
(Chuh-nuun suhl mott ham-nee-dah) 저는 술 못합니다.

Let's go to a karaoke place.
Norae bang euro kapshida.
(No-ray-bahng euroh kahp-she-dah) 노래방으로 갑시다.

What time shall we meet?
Myoshie mannalkkayo?
(Myuh-she-eh mahn-nahl-kah-yoh?) 몇시에 만날까요?

water   *mul (muhl)* 물

bottled water	*saengsu (sang-suu)* 생수
mineral water	*yakssu (yahk-suu)* 약수
coffee	*kopi (koh-pee)* 커피
coffeeshop	*kopi shyop (koh-pee shyop)* 커피숍
tea	*cha (chah)* 차
green tea	*nok cha (no-k chah)* 녹차
milk	*uyu (uu-yuu)* 우유
cocktail	*kakteil (cocktail)* 칵테일
beer	*maekchu (make-juu)* 맥주 / *pio (bee-ah)* 비어
whiskey	*wisuki (whis-kee)* 위스키
wine	*wain (wah-in)* 와인, *podoju (buh-doh-juu)* 포도주

makkoli (mahk-koh-lee) 막걸리: an inexpensive milky wine made from rice and barley; the working man's drink for a long time

makkoli jip (mahk-koh-lee jeep) 막걸리 집: a bar or tavern specializing in this drink

Water, please.
Mul, chushipshio. (Muhl, chuu-ship-she-oh) 물 주십시오.

Coffee, please.
Kopi, chushipshio. (Koh-pee, chuu-ship-she-oh)
커피 주십시오.

Beer, please.
Pio, chushipshio. (Bee-ah, chuu-ship-she-oh)
맥주 주십시오.

Cheers!   *Konbae! (Kom-bay!)* 건배!

The Korean Drinking Culture
The drinking culture in Korea can be considered their "nightlife" because most Korean bars open late from 5 p.m. and stay open till the next morning. Regardless of age or sex, most people enjoy this nightlife. After work, people get together and drink through the night. When young Koreans drink, they play games by singing a song for each round of drink (every drinking game has its own theme song). If one loses a game he/she will drink up as a penalty. The Korean singer Psy's music video for the song "Hangover" is a good example of the Korean drinking culture in action.

65 Bill / Receipt *Kyesanso* (Kay-sahn-suh) / *Yongsujung* (Yuung-suu-juung) 영수증

Please bring me my bill.
Kyesanso-rul juseyo. (Kay-sahn-suh-ruhl juu-say-yoh)
계산서를 주세요.

Let me settle the bill.
Kyesan-un chega hagessumnida. (Kay-sahn-uun cheh-gah hah-gay-sume-nee-dah) 계산은 제가 하겠습니다.

Come on, I'm paying!
Cha, chega sagessumnida! (Chah, cheh-gah sah-geh-sume-nee-dah!) 자, 제가 사겠습니다!

A receipt, please.
Yongsujung chuseyo. (Yuung-suu-juung chuu-say-yoh)
영수증 주세요.

66 Phone *Chonwha* (Chune-whah) 전화

public telephone	*kongjung chonwha* (kong-juung chune-whah) 공중전화

house phone	*jeonwha* (*jone-whah*) 전화
telephone number	*chonhwa ponho* (*chune-hwah bahn-hoh*) 전화번호
telephone directory	*chonwha ponhobu* (*chune-whah bahn-hoe-buu*) 전화번호부
overseas call	*kukje chonwha* (*kuuk-jay chune-whah*) 국제전화
long-distance call	*shioe chonwha* (*she-oh-eh chune-whah*) 시외전화
cell phone	*handu pon* (*hahn-duu pon*) 핸드폰
text message	*munja* (*muun-jah*) 문자
voice mail	*umsong meshiji* (*uhm-suhng-may-she-jee*) 음성 메세지

Where is a public phone?
Kongjung chonhwa ga issoyo? (*Kohng-juung chune-whah-gah ee-suh-yoh?*) 공중전화가 있어요?

I want to make a local call.
Shinae chonhwa-rul hago shippundeyo.
(*She-nay chune-whah-ruhl hah-go ship-puun-day-yoh*)
시내 전화를 하고 싶은데요.

I want to make an international call.
Kukjje chonhwa rul hago shippundeyo.
(*Kuuk-jay chune-whah ruhl hah-go ship-puun-day-yoh*)
국제전화를 하고 싶은데요.

I want to make a collect call.
Sushin-in chibul chonhwa rul hago shippundeyo.
(*Suu-sheen een chee-buhl chune-whah ruhl hah-go ship-puun-day-yoh*) 수신인 지불 전화를 하고 싶은데요.

May I have your phone number?
Chonwha ponho rul chushigesseoyo?
(Chune-whah bohn-hoh ruhl chuu-she-geh-say-oh-yoh?)
전화번호를 주시겠어요?

I would like to rent a cell phone.
Hand pon-rul pilligo shipsumnida.
(Hah-duu pohn-ruhl peel-lee-go ship-sume-nee-dah)
핸드폰을 빌리고 싶습니다.

I want to buy a cell phone.
Hand pon-rul sago shipsumnida.
(Hahn-duu pohn-ruhl sah-go ship-sume-nee-dah)
핸드폰을 사고 싶습니다.

What is your cell phone number?
Handu pon ponhoga mwoyeyo?
(Hahn-duu pohn bohn-hoh-gah mwah-yay-yoh?)
핸드폰 번호가 뭐예요?

My battery is low.
Boetoriga opsoyo. (Baa-toh-ree-gah up-suh-yoh)
배터리가 없어요.

Can I charge my cell phone here?
Yogi-seo Handu pon chung jun halsu issoyo?
(Yoh-ghee seh-oh Hahn-duu pohn chung-juhn hahl-suu ee-suh-yoh?) 여기서 핸드폰 충전할 수 있어요?

My cell phone is not working.
Handu poni kojang nasseoyo.
(Hah-duu pohn-ee koh-jahng nahs-say-oh-yoh)
핸드폰이 고장났어요.

Please send me a text message.
Munja chuseyo. (Munn-jah-chuu-say-yoh) 문자 주세요.

Did you check your voice mail?
Umsong meshiji cheku haesoyo? (Uhm-suhng-may-she-jee check hay-suh-yoh?) 음성 메세지 체크 했어요?

67 Computer *Kompyuto* (Kohm-pyuu-tah) 컴퓨터

laptop   *notubuk (no-tu-buuk)* 노트북

I'd like to use a computer.
Kompyuto-rul ssugo shipundeyo. (*Kome-pyuu-tuh-ruhl suh-go she-puun-day-yoh*) 컴퓨터를 쓰고 싶은데요.

May I borrow a computer?
Kompyuto chom pillyo chushigessum nikka?
(*Kohm-pyuu-tah chome peel-l'uuh chuu-she-guh-sume nee-kkah?*) 컴퓨터를 좀 빌려주시겠습니까?

Where can I plug in my laptop?
Che notubugul yon-gyohalsu innun goshi issoyo?
(*Cheh no-tu-buuk-uhl yun gulh-hahl-suu een-nuhn go-she ee-suh-yoh?*) 제 노트북을 연결할 수 있는 곳이 있어요?

My laptop is not working.
Notubuki kojang nasseoyo. (*No-tu-buuk-ee koh-jahng nahs-say-oh-yoh*) 노트북이 고장났어요.

68 Internet *Intonet* (In-tah-net-tu) 인터넷

Internet café/   *Intonet kape (In-ter-net-tu*
  cybercafé   *kah-pay)* 인터넷 카페

Also:

                       Pishi-Bang (pee-she bahng) 피시
                       방 literally, PC room
modem   *moden* 모뎀

Can I use Wifi?
Wifi dwae yo? (Wai-fai dway yoh?) 와이파이 돼요?

What is your Wifi ID and password?
Wifi ID hago pimil ponhoga ottoke dwaeyo? (Wai-fai ID ha-goh pee-mil-bohn-hoh-gah uht-tuh-kay dway yoh?)
와이파이 아이디하고 비밀번호가 어떻게 돼요?

69 Email *Imeil* (Ee-mail) 이메일

I'd like to send an email.
Imeil-rul ponaeryogo hanundeyo.
(Ee-mail-ruhl poh-nay-re-yoh-guh hah-nuun-day-yoh)
이메일을 보내려고 하는데요.

I'd like to check my email.
Imeil hwagin haryogo hanundeyo.
(E-mail hwah-geen hah-re-yoh-guh hah-nuun-day-yoh)
이메일 확인하려고 하는데요.

What is your email address?
Emeil chuso-ga ottoke dwae yo? (Ee-mail juu-suh-gah uht-tuh-kay dway yoh?) 이메일 주소가 어떻게 돼요?

70 Shopping *Syoping* (Shope-peeng) 쇼핑

shopping center	*syoping sento (shope-peeng sen-tah)* 쇼핑 센터
shop (store)	*kage (kah-gay)* 가게
department store	*paekhwa jom (pake-whah jome)* 백화점
open-air market	*shijang (she-jahng)* 시장
South Gate Market (Seoul)	*Namdaemun Shijang (Nahm-day-muun She-jahng)* 남대문 시장

East Gate Market (Seoul)	*Tongdaemun Shijang* (*Tohng-day-muun She-jahng*) 동대문 시장
Gwangjang Market (Seoul)	*Gwangjang Shijang* (*Gwang-jahng She-jahng*) 광장 시장
Noryangjin Fish Market (Seoul)	*Noryangjin Sosan Shijang* (*Noh-ryahng-jeen Soo-sahn She-jahng*) 노량진 수산 시장

* These markets, called *shijang* (*she-jahng*) 시장, sell everything from fruits and vegetables to shoes, clothes, beddings and traditional pottery. It is customary to haggle with the vendors for better prices. If you intend to do grocery shopping or get a light snack, visit department stores that include a whole basement floor that has a huge grocery section in a supermarket. A large food court is usually found in the basement too. Gwangjang Market is especially famous for its various street foods.

gift shop	*kinyom pum kage* (*kee-yome pume kah-gay*) 기념품 가게
tax-free goods	*myon-se pum* (*m'yone-say pume*) 면세품
price	*kagyok* (*kahg-yoke*) 가격
receipt	*yongsujung* (*yohng-sue-juung*) 영수증
drugstore	*yakkuk* (*yahk-kuuk*) 약국
credit card	*kuredit kadu* (*kuu-reh-deet kah-duu*) 크레디트 카드
Visa Card	*Pija Kadu* (*Bee-jah Kah-duu*) 비자 카드
Master Card	*Masuta Kadu* (*Mahs-tah Kah-duu*) 마스타 카드

I want to go shopping.
Syoping kago shipsumnida. (*Shope-peeng kah-go ship-sume-nee-dah*) 쇼핑 가고 싶습니다.

Where is the nearest department store?
Cheil kakkaun paekwa jom i odi issoyo?
(*Chale kahk-kah-uun pake-wah juhm i ad-dee ee-suh-yoh?*)
제일 가까운 백화점이 어디있어요?

Where is the nearest (open air) market?
Cheil kakkaun shijang ga odi issoyo?
(*Chale kahk-kah-uun she-jahng ad-dee ee-suh-yoh?*)
제일 가까운 시장 어디있어요?

Where is the nearest craft shop?
Cheil kakkaun kongyepum kage ga odi issoyo?
(*Chale kahk-kah-uun kong-yeh-puum kah-gay ga-ad-dee-ee-suh-yoh?*) 제일 가까운 공예품 가게가 어디 있어요?

How much is this?
Igo eol mayeyo? (*Ee-kuu eh-ohl mah-yay-oh?*)
이거 얼마예요?

Can I get a refund?
Hwanbul hago shipundeyo. (*Hwahn-buhl hah-go ship-uhn-deh-yoh*) 환불하고 싶은데요.

Can I exchange this jeans?
Ichungpajirul kyohwan halsu issoyo?
(*Ee- chung-pah-jee-ruhl k'yoh-won hahl-suu ee-sah-yoh?*)
이 청바지를 교환할 수 있어요?

Here is the receipt.
Yogi yongsujungi issumnida. (*Yuh-ghee yuung-suu-juung-ee eesum-nee-dah*) 여기 영수증이 있습니다.

I'm tired.
Pigon haeyo. *(Pee-gohn hay-yoh)* 피곤해요.

Let's take a rest.
Chom shwipshida. *(Chome shweep she-dah)* 좀 쉽시다.

Sales *Seil* *(Sale)* 세일

discount   *harin* *(hah-reen)* 할인 / *enuri* *(ee-nuu-ree)*
                 에누리

Are there any sales going on now?
Chigum seil hanun koshi issumnikka?
(Chee-guhm sale hah-nuun koh-she ee-sume-nee-kah?)
지금 세일 하는 곳이 있습니까?

Are you having a sale?
Chigum seil hanun chung imnika? *(Chee-guum sale hah-nuun chuung eem-nee-kah?)* 지금 세일 하는 중입니까?

That price is too high!
Nomu pissayo! *(No-muu pee-sah-yoh!)* 너무 비싸요!

Can you give me a discount?
Harinhae chushigessumnikka? *(Hah-reen-hay chuu-she-guh-sume-nee-kah?)* 할인해 주시겠습니까?

Please give me a discount!
Kka-kka chuseyo. *(Kah-kah chuu-say-yoh)* 깍아주세요.

I'll give you _____ .
_____ durilkkeyo. *(_____ duh-reel-keh-yoh)*
드릴께요.

Do you have anything cheaper?
Tossan gotto issoyo? (*Tuh-sahn gut-toh ee-suh-yoh?*)
더 싼 것도 있어요?

Clothes *Ot* (*Ot*) 옷

* In Korean, different verbs have to be used for different items of clothing.

t-shirt	*t-shirt* (*t-shirt*)	티셔츠
y-shirt	*y-shirt* (*y-shirt*)	와이셔츠
pants	*paji* (*pah-jee*)	바지
blue jeans	*chungpaji* (*chung-pah-jee*)	청바지
skirt	*chima* (*chee-mah*)	치마

Wear (t-shirt/y-shirt/pants/jeans/skirt)
_____ *ipoyo* (_____ *eep-uh-yoh*)
_____ 입어요.

Can I try this (t-shirt/y-shirt/pants/jeans/skirt)?
Ipaubado dwaeyo? (*Eep-uh bah-doh-dway-yoh?*)
입어 봐도 돼요?

Take off (t-shirt/y-shirt/pants/jeans/skirt)
_____ *bosoyo.* (_____ *buh-suu-yoh*)
_____ 벗어요.

hat	*moja* (*moh-jah*)	모자
glasses	*ankyung* (*ahn-kyung*)	안경
umbrella	*wusan* (*wuu-shan*)	우산

Wear (hat/glasses)
_____ *sseoyo.* (_____ *show-yoh*) _____ 써요.

Can I try this (hat/glasses)?
Sseobado dwaeyo? (*Show bah-doh-dway-yoh?*)
써 봐도 돼요?

Take off (hat/glasses)
_____*bosoyo.* (_____ *buh-suu-yoh*)
_____벗어요.

socks	*yangmal* (*yhang-mahl*)	양말
shoes	*sinbal* (*shin-pal*)	신발
sneakers	*wundonghwa* (*wun-dong-hwa*)	운동화
dress shoes	*kudu* (*kuh-duh*)	구두

Put on (socks/shoes/sneakers/dress shoes)
_____*shinoyo* (_____ *sheen-uh-yoh*)
_____신어요.

Can I try this (socks/shoes/sneakers/dress shoes)?
Shinobado dwaeyo? (*Sheen-uh bah-doh-dway-yoh?*)
신어 봐도 돼요?

Take off (socks/shoes/sneakers/dress shoes)

_____ *bosoyo* (_____ *buh-suu-yoh*)

_____ 벗어요.

earrings   *kwiguri* (*kwee-guhl-ee*) 귀걸이
ring   *panji* (*phan-jee*) 반지
gloves   *jangab* (*jhang-ghab*) 장갑

Put on (earrings/ring/gloves)

_____ *kkyoyo* (_____ *k'yoh-yoh*)

_____ 껴요.

Can I try this (earrings/ring/gloves)?

Kkyobado dwaeyo? (*K'yoh bah-doh-dway-yoh?*)

껴 봐도 돼요?

Take off (earrings/ring/gloves)

_____ *bbayo* (_____ *bbay-yoh*) _____ 빼요.

necklace   *mokguli* (*mokk-guhl-ee*) 목걸이

Put on a necklace.

Mokgulirul haeyo. (*Mokk-guhl-ee-ruhl hay-yoh*)

목걸이를 해요.

Can I try this necklace?

Mokgulirul haebado dwaeyo? (*Mokk-guhl-ee-ruhl hay-bah-doh-dway-yoh?*) 목걸이를 해 봐도 돼요?

Take off a necklace.

Mokgulirul puloyo. (*Mokk-guhl-ee-ruhl puul-uh-yoh*)

목걸이를 풀어요.

watch   *shigae* (*shee-gae*) 시계

Put on a watch.
Shigaerul chayo. (Shee-gae-ruhl chah-yoh) 시계를 차요.

Can I try this watch?
Shigaerul chabado dwaeyo? (Shee-gae-ruhl chah bah-doh-dway-yoh?) 시계를 차 봐도 돼요?

Take off a watch.
Shigaerul puloyo. (Shee-gae-ruhl puul-uh-yoh)
시계를 풀어요.

How do I look?
Otteyo? (ah-ttay-yoh?) 어때요?

It looks good on you.
Chal oullyo yo. (Chal uh-uhl-lay-oh-yoh) 잘 어울려요.

It is good.
Choayo. (Choh-ah-yoh) 좋아요.

It is not good.
Byolroyeyo. (B'yohl-roh-yay-yoh) 별로예요.

It is ok.
Goenchanayo. (Goehn-chahn-ah-yoh) 괜찮아요.

_____ too small.
_____ *nomu chakkayo.* (_____ no-muu chack-ah-yoh) _____ 너무 작아요.

_____ too big.
_____ *nomu kuyo.* (_____ no-muu kuh-yoh) _____너무 커요.

Color Sak (Saek) 색, Sakal (Saekkal) 색깔

* Both words for "color" have the same meaning; **sak** 색 is a Sino-Korean word while **sakal** 색깔 is a native Korean word.

red	**palgansak** (ppal-kkan-saek) 빨간색, **juk** (jeok) 적, **hong** (hohng) 홍
orange	**johwangsak** (juu-hwang-saek) 주황색
yellow	**noransak** (noh-rahn-saek) 노란색, **hwang** (hwahng) 황
green	**noksak** (nok-saek) 녹색, **choroksak** (choh-rok-saek) 초록색
blue	**paransak** (pa-rahn-saek) 파란색, **cheong** (cheohng) 청
navy	**namsak** (nahm-saek) 남색
purple	**borasak** (bo-rah-saek) 보라색
white	**hayansak** (hah-yahn-saek) 하얀색, **hinsak** (hin-saek) 흰색, **baek** (bak) 백
black	**gumensak** (geo-meun-saek) 검은색, **kamansak** (kkah-mahn-saek) 까만색, **heuk** (huk) 흑
gray	**hoesak** (hoe-saek) 회색
brown	**galsak** (ghal-saek) 갈색
pink	**bunhongsak** (bun-hohng-saek) 분홍색

* Koreans abbreviate the colors found in a rainbow: 빨주노초파남보 **paljonochopanambo** (ppal-juu-noh-choh-pa-nahm-bo)

What color do you like most?
Musun sakul cheil choahaseyo? (Muu-suun saek-uhl chale choh-ah-hah-say-yoh?) 무슨 색을 제일 좋아하세요?

What colors do you have?
Musun saki issoyo? *(Muu-suun saek-ee ee-suh-yoh?)*
무슨 색이 있어요?

Can you show me that red hat?
Chu ppal-kan-saek moja chom boyu chuseyo.
(chuh ppal-kan-saek moh-jah choam bo-yuh-chuu-say-yoh)
저 빨간색 모자 좀 보여주세요.

---

74   Post Office *Uche Guk* *(Uu-cheh Guuk)* 우체국

central post office	*jungang uche guk* *(juun-ahng uu-cheh guuk)* 중앙우체국
international parcel post office	*kukje sopo uche guk* *(kuuk-jay sope-oh uu-cheh guuk)* 국제 소포 우체국
letter	*pyonji* *(pyahn-jee)* 편지
postage	*uphyon yogum* *(uu-pyahn yoh-guhm)* 우편 요금
stamp	*uphyo* *(uu-pyah)* 우표
airmail	*hanggong uphyon* *(hahng-goon uu-pyahn)* 항공 우편
surface mail	*sonbak uphyon* *(sahn-bahk uu-pyuhn)* 선박 우편
foreign mail	*oegug uphyon* *(way-guug uu-pyuhn)* 외국 우편
registered mail	*tunggi uphyon* *(tuung-ghee uu-pyuhn)* 등기우편
express mail	*soktal* *(soak-tahl)* 속달
parcel post	*sop'o* *(sope-oh)* 소포
printed matter	*inswae mul* *(en-sway-muhl)* 인쇄물
address	*juso* *(juu-soh)* 주소

return address	**palshinin juso** (*pahl-sheen-een juu-soh*) 발신인 주소
P.O. Box	**Sa Seo Ham** (*Sah Say-oh Hahm*) 사서함
envelope	**pongtu** (*pong-tuu*) 봉투

I want to mail a letter.
Pyonji-rul puchigoshipuhyo. (*P'yohn-jee ruhl puu-chee-go ship-uh-yoh*) 편지를 부치고 싶어요.

Where can I get this wrapped?
Pojang-ha nun tega eodi isseoyo?
(*Poh-jahng ha nuun tay-gah ah-dee ees-say-oh-yoh?*)
포장하는 데가 어디 있어요?

How long does it take to the U.S.?
Miguk kaji olmana kollyo yo?
(*Mee-guuk kah-jee ohl-mah-nah kohl-lay-oh-yoh?*)
미국까지 얼마나 걸려요?

---

75 Hospital *Pyongwon* (*P'yuung-wun*) 병원

dentist	**chikkwa** (*Cheek-kwah*) 치과
pharmacy	**yakkuk** (*yahk-kuuk*) 약국
doctor	**uisa** (*we-sah*) 의사, **uisa sonsaeng nim** (*we-sah sun-sang neem*) 의사 선생님
nurse	**kanhosa** (*kahn-hoh-sah*) 간호사
patient	**hwanja** (*hwahn-jah*) 환자

---

76 Ill / Sick *Pyong* (*P'yohng*) 병

| allergy | **allerugi** (*ahl-ehh-ruh-ghee*) 알레르기 |

107

appendicitis	*maengjangyom (mang-jahng-yuhm)* 맹장염
cough	*kichimul haeyo (kee-chee-muhl hay-yoh)* 기침을 해요
diarrhea	*solsarul haeyo (suhl-sah-ruhl hay-yoh)* 설사를 해요
food poisoning	*shik chungdo-ge kollyossoyo (sheek chuung-doh-gay kuhl-lyuh-ssuh-yoh)* 식중독에 걸렸어요
fever	*yori issoyo (yuh-ree ee-ssuh-yoh)* 열이 있어요
headache	*tudongi issoy (tuu-tohng-ee ee-ssuh-yoh)* 두통이 있어요
heart	*shimjang (sheem-jahng)* 심장
heart attack	*shimjang mabi (sheem-jahng mah-bee)* 심장마비
high fever	*koyol (koh-yuhl)* 고열
runny nose	*kotmuli nawayo (khot-muhl-ee na-wah-yoh)* 콧물이 나와요
sneeze	*jaechaegirul haeyo (jay-chae-gee-ruhl hay-yoh)* 재채기를 해요
stomachache	*paega apayo (pay-gah ah-pah-yoh)* 배가 아파요
toothache	*chitong-i issoyo (Chee-tohng-ee ee-ssuh-yoh)* 치통이 있어요

I feel (am) sick.
Momi apumnida. (Moh-me ah-pume-nee-dah)
몸이 아픕니다.

OR:

Momi apayo. (Moh-me ah-pah-yoh) 몸이 아파요.

I'm sick.
Pyong-i nasseoyo. (P'yohng-ee nahs-say-oh-yoh)
병이 났어요.

I've got a bad cold.
Chonun shimhan kamgie kollyossumnida.
(Chuh-nuun sheem-hahn kahm-ghee-eh kohl-yuh sume-nee-dah) 저는 심한 감기에 걸렸습니다.

I have a bad headache.
Chonun tutong-i maeu shimhamnida.
(Chuh-nuun tuu-dohng ee may-uu sheem-hahm-nee-dah)
저는 두통이 매우 심합니다.

Please send for a doctor.
Uisa-rul pulro chuseyo.
(We-sah-ruhl puhl-roh chuu-say-yoh) 의사를 불러주세요.

I have a toothache.
Nanun iga apayo. (Nah-nuun ee-gah ah-pah-yoh)
나는 이가 아파요.

I've lost a filling.
Pong-i bajo ssoyo. (Pong-ee bah-juh suh-yoh)
봉이 빠졌어요.

I need to go to a dentist.
Chikwae kago chipssumnida. (Cheek-kway kah-go chip-sume-nee-dah) 치과에 가고 싶습니다.

Do you know a dentist who speaks English?
Yong-o rul malha-nun chikwauisa-rul ashimnikka?
(Yohng-ah ruhl mahl-hah-nuun chee-kwa-we-sah-ruhl ah-sheem-nee-kah?) 영어를 말하는 치과의사를 아십니까?

I want to make an appointment with the dentist.
Ku chikkwa-e ye yak-ul hago shipundeyo.
(*Kuu cheek-wah-eh yahk-ruhl hah-go ship-uhn-deh-yoh*)
그 치과에 예약을 하고싶은데요.

77 Body *Mom* (*Mohm*) 몸

head	*meori* (*muh-ree*) 머리	
face	*eolgul* (*ahl-guhl*) 얼굴	
eye	*nun* (*nuun*) 눈	
ear	*kwi* (*kwee*) 귀	
nose	*ko* (*koh*) 코	
lip	*ip* (*eep*) 입	
neck	*mok* (*moke*) 목	
shoulder	*eokae* (*uh-kay*) 어깨	
arm	*pal* (*pahl*) 팔	
hand	*son* (*sohn*) 손	
finger	*songarak* (*sohn-gah-rak*) 손가락	
stomach	*pae* (*pay*) 배	
waist	*heori* (*huh-ree*) 허리	
leg	*dari* (*dah-ree*) 다리	
knee	*mureup* (*muu-rup*) 무릎	
foot	*bal* (*bahl*) 발	
toe	*balgarak* (*bahl-gah-rak*) 발가락	

78 Emergencies *Pisang Sangtae* (*Pee-sahng Sang-tay*) 비상 상태

ambulance	*ambyullonsu* (*ambulance*) 앰블런스 / *kugupcha* (*kuu-guup-chah*) 구급차
injury (wound)	*pusang* (*puu-sahng*) 부상
cut, bruise	*sangcho* (*sahng-choh*) 상처

severe wound	*chung sang* (*chuung sahng*) 중상
hurt	*dachida* (*dah-chee-dah*) 다치다
break	*purojida* (*puu-ruh-jee-dah*) 부러지다
help! (call for)	*towa chuseyo!* (*toh-wah chuu-say-yoh!*) 도와주세요!
heart attack	*shimjang mabi* (*sheem-jahng mah-bee*) 심장마비
emergency exit	*pisang gu* (*pee-sahng guu*) 비상구

I've been hurt!
Chega tacho sseo yo! (*Chay-gah tah-choh say-oh yoh!*)
제가 다쳤어요!

I broke my leg!
Dariga purojosse oyo! (*Dah-ree-gah puu-ruh-juh suh-yoh*) 다리가 부러졌어요!

Please call an ambulance!
Kugupcha chom pullol chuseyo!
(*Kuu-guup-chah chome puhl-yohl chuu-say-yoh!*)
구급차 좀 불러주세요!

Please call an ambulance quickly!
Ppalli kugupcha rul pullo chuseyo!
(*Bahl-lee kuu-guup- chah ruhl puhl-lah chuu-say-yoh!*)
빨리 구급차를 불러 주세요!

I cannot speak Korean.
Hangugma-reul mot hae-yo.
(*Hahn-guuk-mah-ruhl mote hay-yoh*) 한국말을 못 해요.

Is there anyone who can speak English?
Yong-o rul ha-nun saram issumnikka?
(*Yohng-ah ruhl hah-nuun sah-rahm ee-sume-nee-kah?*)
영어를 하는 사람 있습니까?

I am disabled.
Chon chang-aein indeyo.
(*Chohn chahng-aa-een een-day-yoh*) 전 장애인 인데요.

Is there wheelchair access?
Hwilcheo churipkuga issoyo? (*Wheel cheh-ah chuu-reep-kuu-gah ee-ssuh-yoh?*) 휠체어 출입구가 있어요?

Fire! [shout in case of fire]
Puriya! (*Buu-ree-yah!*) 불이야!

Help! [shout in a life-threatening situation]
Towa juseyo! (*Doh-wah juu-say-yoh!*) 도와 주세요!

Watch out! [when danger threatens]
Choshim haeyo! (*Choh-sheem hay-yoh!*) 조심해요!

I'm lost!
Ki-rul irossoyo! (*Kee-ruhl ee-ruh-ssuh-yoh!*)
길을 잃었어요!

Would you please help me?
Chom towa chushige sumnikka? (*Chome tow-wah chuu-she-geh sume-nee-kah?* 좀 도와 주시겠습니까?

May I use your telephone?
Chonhwa chom sseodo doelkkayo? (*Chune-whah chome show-doh dohl-kah yoh?*) 전화 좀 써도 될까요?

Haircut *Ibal* *(Ee-bahl)* 이발

barbershop	*ibalsso* *(ee-bahl-ssah)* 이발소
barber	*ibalsa* *(ee-bahl-sah)* 이발사
beauty salon	*mijang won* *(me-jahng wahn)* 미장원
hairdresser	*miyongsa* *(me-yohng-sah)* 미용사
hair set	*mori setu* *(muh-ree say-tuu)* 머리 세트
shampoo	*shyampu* *(shahm-puu)* 샴푸
perm	*pama* *(pha-mah)* 파마 해요
dye	*yomsak* *(yuhm-saek)* 염색 해요
trim	*dadumoyo* *(dah-dum-uh-yoh)* 다듬어요

Is there a barbershop in the hotel?
Hotel-e ibalsso-ga issumnikka? (Hotel eh ee-bahl-ssah-ga ee-sume-nee-kah?) 호텔에 이발소가 있습니까?

How much for a haircut?
Mori hanun de olma jiyo? (Much-ree-hah-nuun-day ohl-mah-jee-yoh?) 머리하는데 얼마지요?

Just a trim, please. [for guys only]
Chogum man kka-kka chuseyo. (Choh-guum mahn kah-kah chuu-say-yoh) 조금만 깍아주세요.

Just a trim, please.
Chogum man dadumo chuseyo. (Choh-guum mahn dah-dum-uh chuu-say-yoh) 조금만 다듬어 주세요.

Is there a beauty salon in the hotel?
Hotel-e mijang won i isseoyo? (Hotel eh me-jahng wahn i ees-say-yoh?) 호텔에 미장원이 있어요?

I would like to have my hair set.
Morirul setuhae chusaeyo. *(Muh-ree-ruhl say-tuu-hay chuu-say-yoh)* 머리를 세트 해 주세요.

A shampoo, please.
Shyampu, hae chusaeyo. *(Shahm-puu hay chuu-say-yoh)* 샴푸 해 주세요.

Dry my hair, please.
Durai hae chushipshio. *(Duu-rye hay chuu-say-yoh)* 드라이 해 주세요.

OR:

Morirul malrya chusaeyo. *(Mahl-r'yaw chuu-say-yoh)* 머리를 말려 주세요.

I would like to have a perm.
Pamarul hago shipundeyo. *(Pah-mah-ruhl hah-go ship-uhn-deh-yoh)* 파마를 하고 싶은데요.

How long does it take?
Olmana kollyo yo? *(Ohl-mah-nah kohl-lay-oh-yoh?)* 얼마나 걸려요?

Sightseeing *Kwangwang* *(Kwahn-gwahng)* 관광 / *Kugyong* *(Kuu-g'yohng)* 구경

travel	*yohaeng* *(yuh-hang)* 여행
vacation	*bang hak* *(bahng hahk)* 방학
holiday	*hyuga* *(hyuu-gah)* 휴가
far	*mon* *(mun)* 먼; *molli* *(muhl-lee)* 멀리
close	*kakkaun* *(kahk-kah-uun)* 가까운

sightseeing bus	***kwangwang bosu*** *(kwahn-gwahng buh-suu)* 관광버스
tourist information office	***kwangwang annaeso*** *(kwahn gwahn ahn-nay-soh)* 관광 안내소
tourist spot	***kwangwang myongso*** *(kwahn-gwahng m'yung-soh)* 관광 명소
Korean Folk Village	***Minsok Chon*** *(Meen-soak Chuhn)* 민속촌
Kyungbok Palace	***Kyongbok Kung*** *(K'yohng-bok Kuung)* 경복궁
Great South Gate*	***Namdaemun*** *(Nahm-day-muun)* 남대문

* Seoul's most famous gate, ranked as Korea's Number 1 National Treasure.

The Blue House*	***Chongwa Dae*** *(Chohng-wah Day)* 청와대

* The President's Residence

Panmunjom*	***Panmunjom*** *(Pahn-muun-jome)* 판문점

* The DMZ Command Grounds

border (of country)	***Kukggyong*** *(Kuke-kyahng)* 국경

* Famous Seoul city tour spots: Kyungbok Palace, Changdeok Palace, Deoksu Palace, Changgyeong Palace, Jogye Buddhist Temple, Insadong Antique street, Nam-sangol Hanok Village, Namsan Seoul Tower, Cheonggye Stream and Great South Gate Market.

Do you have any plan for the holidays?
Hyuga tae musun kyehoek issuseyo?
(*Hyuu-gah-tay muu-suhn kay-hoak ee-suu-say-yoh?*)
휴가때 무슨 계획 있으세요?

What will you do this vacation?
Bang hak tae mwo halguyeyo? (*Bahng-hahk-tay mwah hahl-guh-yay-yoh?*) 방학 때 뭐 할거예요?

I want to go sightseeing.
Kwangwang hago shipsupnida. (*Kwahn-gwahng hah-go ship-suup-nee-dah*) 관광하고 싶습니다.

Where is the most popular tourist spot at Seoul?
Seouleso cheil youmyonghan kwangwang myongsoga odie issoyo? (*Seoul-ee-soh chale yuu-m'yung-hahn kwahn-gwahng m'yung-soh-gah ah-dee-eh ee-suh-yoh?*) 서울에서 제일 유명한 관광 명소가 어디에 있어요?

Where is a/the tourist information office?
Kwangwang annaeso ga odi issoyo?
(*Kwahn-gwahn ahn-nay-soh gah ah-dee ee-suh yoh?*)
관광 안내소 가 어디 있어요?

Can I take a bus to the Korean Folk Village?
Minsok Chon-e pposeo-ro kal su issoyo?
(*Meen-soak Chohn-eh poh-suh-roh kahl suu ee-suh-yoh?*)
민속촌에 버스로 갈 수 있어요?

Can I go to Jeju Island by ferry?
Cheju Do hang bae-ga issoyo? (*Cheh-juu Doh hang bae-gah ee-soh-yoh?*) 제주도행 배가 있어요?

I would like to go to Namdaemun.
Namdaemun-e kago shipsumneda. (Nahm-day-muun-eh kah-go ship-sume-nee-dah) 남대문에 가고 싶습니다.

Please take me to Namdaemun.
Namdaemun-eu-ro chom kachuseyo.
(Nahm-day-muun-yuu-roh chome kah-chuu-say-yoh)
남대문으로 좀 가주세요.

Where is the Blue House?
Chongwa Dae-ga odiso soh-yoh?
(Chohng-wah Day-gah ad-dee-suh soh-yoh?)
청와대가 어딨어요?

Is the Blue House open to visitors?
Chongwa Dae reul ku-gyong-hal su issoyo?
(Chohng-wah Day ruhl kuu-gyohng-hahl suu ee-soh-yoh?)
청와대를 구경할 수 있어요?

I would like to go to Panmunjom.
Panmunjom-e ka-go shipoyo. (Pahn-muun-jome-e kah-go ship-oh-yoh) 판문점에 가고 싶어요.

How far is the border from here?
Yogi-so kukggyong kkaji olmana momnikka?
(Yah-ghee-sah kuke-kyahng kah-jee ahl-mah-nah mahm-nee-kah?) 여기서 국경까지 얼마나 멉니까?

How far is it from here?
Yogiso olmana moloyo? (Yuh-ghee-suh ohl-mah-nah muhl-uh-yoh?) 여기서 얼마나 멀어요?

The Kyungbok Palace is nearby.
Kyongbok Kungun yogiseo kakkawoyo.
(K'yohng-bok Kuung-eun yoh-ghee-suh kahk-kah-wah-yoh)
경복궁은 여기서 가까워요.

How long does it take to _____?
_____ *kaji olmana olmana kollyo yo?*
(_____ *kah-jee ohl-mah-nah kohl-lay-oh-yoh?*)
_____ 까지 얼마나 걸려요?

Could you take a picture of me?
Saijin chom chigo chushigesseoyo?
(*Sigh-jeen chome chee-guh chuu-she-geh-say-oh-yoh?*)
사진 좀 찍어 주시겠어요?

81 Folk Customs *Pungsup* (*Puung-suhp*) 풍습

folk dance	*minsok muyong* (*meen-soak muu-yohng*) 민속 무용
Korean folk songs	*Hanguk minyo* (*Hahn-guuk meen-yoh*) 한국 민요
Korean dramatic song	*Pansori* (*pahn-soh-ree*) 판소리
crane dance	*hak chum* (*hahk chuum*) 학춤
monk's dance	*sung-mu* (*suhg-muu*) 승무
Korean fan dance	*puchechum* (*puu-chay-chuum*) 부채춤
Korean mask dance	*talchum* (*tahl-chuum*) 탈춤
Korean circle dance play	*kanggangsulae* (*kahng-kahng-suu-uhl-lay*) 강강술래
Korean traditional percussion quartet	*samulnori* (*sah-muhl-no-ree*) 사물놀이

I'm interested in the drum dance.
Changgo chum-e kwanshim-i isseo yo.
(Chahng-go chuum-eh kwahn-sheem-ee ee-say-oh yoh)
장고춤에 관심이 있어요.

What is playing at the Sejong Cultural Center?
Sejong Munwha Hogwan-e seo musun kongyon-i is-seoyo? (Say-johng Muun-whah Hoh-gwahn-eh say-oh muu-suun kong yohn-ee ee-say-oh yoh?)
세종문화회관에서 무슨 공연이 있어요?

I would like to have a recording of Korean folk songs.
Hanguk minyo rekodu-rul han chang sago shipsumnida.
(Hahn-guuk meen-yoh ray-koh-duu-ruhl hahn chahng sah-go ship-sume-nee-dah)
한국 민요레코드를 한 장 사고싶습니다.

Is this a Korean custom?
Igosun Hanguk pungsup imnikka? (Ee-go-suun Hahn-guuk puung-suhp eem-nee-kah?) 이것은 한국 풍습입니까?

---

82   Admission *Ipchang* *(Eep-chahng)* 입장

admission fee   *ipchang nyo (eep-chahng n'yoh)* 입장료
admission   *ipchang kwon (eep-chahng kwun)*
  ticket   입장권

What is the admission fee?
Ipchang nyo-ga olma imnika? (Eep-chanhng n'yoh gah ahl-mah eem-nee-kah?) 입장료가 얼마입니까?

Is it free?
Muryo imnikka? (Muu-rio eem-nee-kah?) 무료입니까?

Avenue / Street *Toro* (Doh-roh) 도로

What is the name of this street?
I toro-e irumi mwoshimnika? (Ee doh-roh-eh ee-ruu-me mwah-sheem-nee-kah?) 이 도로의 이름이 무엇입니까?

Sports *Undong* (Uhn-dong) 운동

baseball	*yagu* (yah-guu)	야구
basketball	*nonggu* (nong-guu)	농구
golf	*kolpu* (kohl-puu)	골프
ice hockey	*aisu haki* (aye-suu hah-kee)	아이스 하키
martial arts	*musul* (muu-suhl)	무술
soccer	*chukku* (chuhk-kuu)	축구
taekwondo	*taekwondo* (tay-kwahn-doh)	태권도
tennis	*tenisu* (tay-nee-suu)	테니스
volleyball	*yoga* (yoh-gah)	요가
swimming	*suyong* (suu-yohng)	수영

Do you like sports?
Undong choahaseyo? (Uhn-dong choh-ah-hah-say-yoh?)
운동 좋아하세요?

What sports do you play?
Musun undong haseyo? (Muu-suhn uhn-dong hah-say-yoh?) 무슨 운동 하세요?

What sports do you follow?
Otton undong-e kwanshimi issuseyo?
(Oat-tone uhn-dong-eh kwahn-she-me ee-suu-say-yoh?)
어떤 운동에 관심이 있으세요?

Do you practice yoga?
Yoga haljul aseyo? (Yoga hahl-juhl ah-say-yoh?)
요가 할 줄 아세요?

Can you ride a bike?
Chajongo taljul aseyo? (Chah-johng-oh tahl-juhl ah-say-yoh?) 자전거 탈 줄 아세요?

Where do you play golf?
Kolpu odiso chiseyo? (Gohl-fuu ah-dee-suh chee-say-yoh?)
골프를 어디서 치세요?

Do you play tennis?
Tenisu chiseyo? (Tay-nee-suu chee-say-yoh?)
테니스 치세요?

Where is the nearest swimming pool?
Kakkaun suyong jangi odi issoyo?
(Kahk-kah-uun suu-yohng-jahng-ee ah-dee ee-suh-yoh?)
가까운 수영장이 어디 있어요?

How much are the green fees?
Yogum-i olma-e yo? (Yoh-guhm-ee ohl-mah-eh yoh?)
요금이 얼마에요?

Hobby *Chwimi* (Ch'we-me) 취미

reading	*doksu (dohk-suh)* 독서	
exercising	*undong (uhn-dong)* 운동	
fishing	*naksi (nahk-shee)* 낚시	
collecting	*mougi (moh-ui-ghee)* 모으기	
watching movies	*yonghwa kamsang (yohng-hwah kahm-sahng)* 영화 감상	

listening to music *umak kamsang* (*uh-mahk kahm-sahng*)
음악 감상

What is your hobby?
Chwimiga mwoyeyo? (*Ch'we-me-gah mwho-yay-yoh?*)
취미가 뭐 예요?

My hobby is reading.
Che chwiminun doksu imnida. (*Cheh ch'we-me-nuun dohk-suh-eem-nee-dah*) 제 취미는 독서입니다.

What do you do in your free time?
Shigan issultae mwo haseyo? (*She-gahn ee-suhl-tay mwoh hah-say-yoh?*) 시간 있을 때 뭐 하세요?

I like to watch movies.
Chunun yonghwa kamsangul choahamnida.
(*Chuh-nuun yohng-hwah kahm-sahng-uhl choh-ah-hahm-nee-dah*) 저는 영화감상을 좋아합니다.

---

86 School *Hakkyo* (*Hahk-k'yoh*) 학교

teacher	*sunsaeng nim* (*sun-sang neem*) 선생님	
professor	*kyosu nim* (*k'yoh-suh-neem*) 교수님	
student	*haksaeng* (*hahk-sang*) 학생	
university student	*taehaksaeng* (tay-hahk-sang) 대학생	
freshman	*shinipsaeng* (*sheen-eep-sang*) 신입생, *il haknyon* (*eel-hahk-n'yuhn*) 일 학년	
sophomore	*i haknyon* (*ee-hahk-n'yuhn*) 이 학년	
junior	*sam haknyon* (*sahm-hahk-n'yuhn*) 삼 학년	
senior	*sa haknyon* (*sah-hahk-n'yuhn*) 사 학년	

student ID card	*haksaengjung (hahk-sang-juung)* 학생증
preschool	*youchiwon (yuu-chee-wun)* 유치원
primary school [six years]	*chodeung hakkyo (choh-dohng hahk-k'yoh)* 초등 학교 *six years
middle school [three years]	*chong hakkyo (chong hakk-k'yoh)* 중학교
high school [three years]	*kodeung hakkyo (koh-duhng)* 고등학교

* In Korea, school years are not counted sequentially from elementary school through high school; counting starts at each school-level. So a senior in an American high school is equivalent to a third-year high school student in Korea.

university	*taehakkyo (tay-hahk-k'yoh)* 대학교
graduate school	*tae hagwon (tay hah-gwon)* 대학원
private school	*sarip hakkyo (sah-reep hahk-k'yoh)* 사립 학교
public school	*gongrip hakkyon (ghong-reep hahk-k'yoh)* 공립 학교
entrance into a school	*iphak (eep-hahk)* 입학
graduate	*cholop (chohl-ope)* 졸업
classroom	*kyoshil (k'yoh-sheel)* 교실
office	*samusil (sah-muh-sheel)* 사무실
desk	*chaeksang (chake-shang)* 책상
table	*takja (tahk-jah)* 탁자
chair	*uuija (we-jah)* 의자
chalkboard	*chilpan (cheel-pahn)* 칠판
homework	*sukjae (suuk-jay)* 숙제

test	*sihom* (she-huum) 시험
question	*chilmun* (cheel-muun) 질문
textbook	*kyokwaso* (k'yoh-kwah-suh) 교과서
notebook	*kongchaek* (khong-chake) 공책
pencil	*yonphil* (yuhn-pheel) 연필
eraser	*jiwogae* (jee-wu-gay) 지우개

Are you still a student?
Ajigdo haksaeng imnikka? (Ah-jeeg-doh hahk-sang eem-nee-kah?) 아직도 학생입니까?

I am a graduate student.
Chunun tae hagwonsaeng imnida. (Chuh-nuun tay hah-gwon-sang eem-nee-dah) 저는 대학원생입니다.

Which university do you attend?
Onu taeha-ge tanishimnikka? (Oh-nuu tay-hah-geh tah-nee-sheem-nee-kah?) 어느 대학에 다니십니까?

Are you a student at Seoul National University?
Soul taehakkyo haksaeng imnikka?
(Sole tay-hahk-k'yoh hahk-sang eem-nee-kah?)
서울대학교 학들입니까?

What are you studying?
Musun kongbu-rul haseyo? (Muu-suhn kong-buu-ruhl hah-say-yoh?) 무슨 공부를 하세요?

Which university did you graduate from?
Onu taeha-gul choropaessumnikka?
(Oh-nuu tay-hah-guhl choh-rope-pay-sume-nee-kah?)
어느 대학을 졸업했습니까?

Professor Kim, I have a question.
Kim kyosu nim chilmun issumnida. (K'yoh-suu-neem cheel-muun e-sume-nee-dah) 김 교수님, 질문 있습니다.

Birthday *Saengil* (Sang-eel) 생일

When is your birthday?
Saeng-iri onje eyo? (Sang-ee-ree uhn-jeh eh-yoh?)
생일이 언제예요?

In which year were you born?
Tangshin-un myon-nyou-do-e taeona sumnika?
(Tahng-sheen-uhn m'yohn-n'yoh-doh-eh tay-uh-nah sume-nee-kah?) 당신은 몇년도에 태어났습니까?

Where were you born?
Odiso taeona sumnikka? (Ah-dee-suh tay-uh-nah sume-nee-kah?) 어디서 태어났습니까?

My birthday is next week.
Che saengil-i taum chu-e issumnida.
(Cheh sang-eel-ee taj-uhm chuu-eh ees-sume-nee-dah)
제 생일이 다음 주에 있습니다.

Congratulations!
Chukahaeyo! (Chuu-kah-hay-yoh!) 축하해요!

Happy birthday!
Saeng-il chukka haeyo! (Sang-eel chuuk-kah hay-yoh!)
생일 축하해요!

My birthday is on _____ .
Che saeng-irun _____ . (Cheh sang-ee-ruhn _____)
제 생일은 _____.

Would you like to come to my birthday party?
Che saeng-il patie oshiji ankessumnikka?
(Cheh sang-eel pah-tee oh-she-jee ahn-keh-sume-nee-kah?)
제 생일 파티에 오시지 않겠습니까?

Let's blow the candles!
Choburul puroyo! (chot-bu-ruhl puu-ruh-yoh)
촛불을 불어요!

Thank you for the present.
Sonmul kamsahamnida. (Suhn-muhl kahm-sah-hahm-nee-dah) 선물 감사합니다.

88 Anniversary *Kinyomil* (Keen-yuh-meel) 기념일

wedding anniversary   *kyorhon kinyomil* (k'yuhr-hone keen-yuh-meel) 결혼 기념일

Today is our anniversary.
Onu-run chohi-dul-ui kinyomil imnida.
(Oh-nuu-ruhn choh-he-duhl-we keen-yoh-meel eem-nee-dah)
오늘은 저희들의 기념일입니다.

89 Movies *Yonghwa* (Yuhng-hwah) 영화

I booked a movie ticket.
Yonghwarul yemae haeseyo. (Yuhng-hwah-ruhl yay-may haht-say-yoh) 영화를 예매했어요.

Let's go see a movie tonight!
Onul chonyoke yonghwarul poro kapshida!
(Oh-nuhl chun-yuk-eh yuhng-hwah-ruhl poh-roh kahp-she-dah) 오늘 저녁에 영화를 보러 갑시다!

What movie is playing?
Yonghwa gwaneso mwol sangyong haeyo?
(Yuhng-hwah gwahn-eh suh mwahl sahng-yuhng hay-yoh?)
영화관에서 뭘 상영해요?

Does it have English subtitles?
Yong-O chamak nawayo? (*Yuhng-Oh chah-mahk nah-wah-yoh?*) 영어 자막나와요?

Two tickets, please.
Tu jang juseyo. (*Tuu jahng juu-say-yoh*) 두 장 주세요.

90 Date (romantic) *Teitu* (*Day-tuu*) 데이트

girlfriend	*yoja chingu* (*yuh-jah cheen-guu*) 여자친구
boyfriend	*namja chingu* (*nahm-jah cheen-guu*) 남자친구
café	*kape* (*kah-peh*) 카페
traditional teahouse	*chongtong chatchibe* (*chohng-tohng chah-chee-beh*) 전통 찻집
nightclub	*naitu* (*nigh-tuu*) 나이트
club	*kullop* (*kuu-lahb*) 클럽
karaoke bar	*norae bang* (*no-ray bahng*) 노래방
"singing rooms" theater	*kukchang* (*kuhk-chahng*) 극장
park	*kongwon* (*kohng-won*) 공원
movie theater	*yonghwa gwan* (*yuhng-hwah gwahn*) 영화관
bookstore	*sojom* (*suh-juum*) 서점
restaurant	*sikttang* (*sheek-dahng*) 식당

What are you doing this evening?
Onul bame mwo haseyo? (*Oh-nuhl bah-meh mwah hah-say-yoh?*) 오늘 밤에 뭐하세요?

How about going out for a drink?
Sul mashiro kalkkayo? *(Suhl mah-she-ruh kahl-kah-yoh?)*
술 마시러 갈까요?

Let's go dancing.
Chumchugo shipoyo. *(Chuum-chuugo ship-uh-yoh)*
춤추고 싶어요.

Would you like to dance?
Chum chushillaeyo? *(Chuum chuu-sheel-lay-yoh?)*
춤 추실래요?

We have a date tomorrow.
Naeil teitu issuminda. *(Nay-ell day-tuu ee-sume-nee-dah)*
내일 데이트 있습니다.

Where shall we meet?
Odiso mannalkkayo? *(Ah-dee-suh mahn-nahl-kah-yoh?)*
어디서 만날까요?

What time shall we meet?
Myoshie mannalkkayo? *(M'yuh-she-eh mahn-nahl-kah-you?)* 몇 시에 만날까요?

What kind of music do you like?
Otton umagul choa haseyo? *(Oat-ton uh-mah-guhl choh-ah hah-say-yoh?)* 어떤 음악을 좋아 하세요?

What kind of food do you like?
Otton umshikul choa haseyo? *(Oat-ton uum-sheek-uhl choh-ah hah-say-yoh?)* 어떤 음식을 좋아 하세요?

May I ring you?
Chonhwa haedo dwaeyo?
(Chone-hwah hay-doh dway-yoh?) 전화 해도 돼요?

May I have your phone number, please?
Chonhwa ponho chom chushigesseoyo?
(Chune-hwah bahn-hoh chome chuu-she-geh-say-oh-yoh?)
전화번호 좀 주시겠어요?

Do you use Facebook?
Facebook haseyo? (Facebook hah-say-yoh?)
페이스 북 하세요?

What is your email address?
Emeil chuso-ga ottoke dwaeyo? (Ee-mail juu-suh-gah uht-tuh-kay dway yoh?) 이메일 주소가 어떻게 돼요?

What is your kakaotalk ID?
Kakaotalk aediga mwoyeyo? (Kakaotalk aye-dee-gah mwho-yay-yoh?) 카카오톡 아이디가 뭐예요?

Can I see you again?
Ddo mannal su ittulkayo? (Ddoh mahn-nahal-suu eet-suhl-kah-yoh?) 또 만날 수 있을 까요?

I like you.
Choahaeyo. (Choh-ah-hay-yoh) 좋아해요.

I love you.
Saranghaeyo. (Sah-rahng-hay-yoh) 사랑해요.

91 Wedding *Kyoron* *(K'yuh-rone)* 결혼

traditional wedding	*chongtong honrae* *(chohng-tohng hone-ray)* 전통 혼례
wedding ceremony	*kyoron shik (K'yuh-rone sheek)* 결혼식

wedding hall	*kyoron shik jang* (*K'yuh-rone sheek jhang*) 결혼식장
wedding reception	*piroyon* (*pee-roh-yun*) 피로연
nuptial song	*chukka* (*chuhk-kah*) 축가
engagement	*yakon* (*yah-kone*) 약혼
bride	*shinbu* (*sheen-buu*) 신부
groom	*shillang* (*sheel-lahng*) 신랑
guest	*hagaek* (*hah-gake*) 하객
wedding cake	*weding keiku* (*weh-deeng kay-kuu*) 웨딩 케이크
wedding present	*kyoron sonmul* (*k'yuh-rone suhn-muhl*) 결혼 선물
honeymoon	*shinhon yohaeng* (*sheen-hone yuh-hang*) 신혼 여행
congratulatory money	*chukuikum* (*chuhk-we-kuhm*) 축의금

Congratulations on your wedding!
Kyoron chukahaeyo! (*K'yuh-rone chuu-kah-hay-yoh!*)
결혼 축하해요!

When is your wedding?
Kyoron shike onjeyeyo?
(*K'yuh-rone sheek-ee ahn-jeh-yay-yoh?*)
결혼식이 언제예요?

Where is the wedding hall?
Kyoron shik jange odiyeyo (*K'yuh-rone sheek jhang-ee ah-dee-yay-yoh?*) 결혼식장이 어디예요?

Where do you go for your honeymoon?
Shinhon yohaeng odiro kayo? (*Sheen-hone yuh-hang ah-dee-ruh kah-yoh?*) 신혼여행 어디로 가요?

Business *Bijinesu* (Bee-jee-nay-suu) 비즈니스

company	*hoesa* (hwaysah) 회사
company employee	*hoesawon* (hwaysahwuhn) 회사원; *chigwonin* (chee-gwuhn-een) 직장인
boss	*sangsa* (shang-sah) 상사
co-worker	*tongyo* (tohng-nryoh) 동료
businessperson	*shaopka* (sha-up-kah) 사업가; *sangin* (sahng-een) 상인
employer	*koyongju* (koh-yohng-juu) 고용주; *chuin* (chuu-een) 주인
staff	*chigwon* (chee-gwuhn) 직원
clerk	*chongupwon* (chong-up-wuhn) 종업원
part-time job	*arubaitu* (ah-ruu-bah-ee-tuu) 아르바이트
occupation	*chigop* (chee-gup) 직업
workplace	*chikjang* (cheek-jahng) 직장
business hours	*yongop shigan* (yuhng-gup she-gahn) 영업시간
go to work	*chulgun* (chuul-guhn) 출근
leave work	*tooegun* (thay-guhn) 퇴근
night overtime	*yagun* (yah-guhn) 야근
join a company	*ipsa* (eep-sah) 입사
resignation	*tooesa* (thay-sah) 퇴사
layoff	*haego* (hay-goh) 해고
day off	*hyuga* (hyuu-gah) 휴가
business trip	*chuljang* (chuhl-jahng) 출장
salary	*wolgup* (wuhl-guup) 월급
annual salary	*yonbong* (yun-bohng) 연봉
get-together*	*hoe-shik* (hway-sheek) 회식

* **Hoe-shik** means that a small group of people from the same company — including fellow associates and managers — get together for dinner and drinks after work. In Korea, there is a tendency to think that a company dinner is also an extension of work. So drinking sessions play a significant role in business relationships. For a detailed explanation, refer to *The Korean Way in Business* (Tuttle Publishing Group)

What do you do?
Musunil haseyo? (muu-suhn-eel hah-say-yoh?)
무슨 일 하세요?

What is your business?
Otton shaop haseyo? (Oat-tone sha-up hah-say-yoh?)
어떤 사업 하세요?

Where is your workplace?
Chikjangi odie issoyo? (Cheek-jahng-ee ah-dee-eh ee-suh-yoh?) 직장이 어디에 있어요?

What time do you go to work?
Myotshie chulgun haseyo? (M'yaht-she-eh chuhl-guhn hah-say-yoh?) 몇 시에 출근 하세요?

I have a meeting today.
Onul hoeuiga issumnida. (Oh-nuhl hwey-we-gah e-sume-neé-dah) 오늘 회의가 있습니다.

Let's get together today!
Onul hoe-shik hapshida! (Oh-nuhl hway-sheek hap-shee-dah!) 오늘 회식합시다!

93 | Agent (Business) *Tairiin (Die-ree-een)* 대리인

real estate	***budongsan** (buu-dong-sahn)* 부동산; ***poktok pang** (poke-toke pahng)* 복덕방
real estate agent	***budongsan jungaein** (buu-dong-sahn juung-gay-in)* 부동산 중개인

I have an agent in Seoul.
***Soul-e tairiin issumnida.** (Sohl-eh dai-ree-een ee-sume-nee-dah)* 서울에 대리인이 있습니다

Do you have an agent in Pusan?
***Busan-e tairiin issumnikka?** (Buu-sahn-eh die-ree-een ee-sume-nee-kah?)* 부산에 대리인이 있습니까?

Would you please recommend a good real estate agent?
***Choun poktok pang-rul sogaehae chushiji ankessumi-nikka?** (Choh-uhn poke-toke pahng-ruhl so-gay-hay chuu-she-jii ahn-keh-sume-nee-kah?)* 좋은 복덕방을 소개해 주시지않겠습니까?

94 | Agreement / Contract *Kyeyak (Kay-yahk)* 계약

house rental agreement	*jutak imdae kyeyak (juh-tak eem-dy kay-yahk)* 주택임대계약
cancel a contract	***kyeyag-ul haejehada** (kay-yahg-uhl hay-jeh-hah-dah)* 계약을 해제하다
make a contract	***kyeyag-ul hada** (kay-yahg-uhl hah-dah)* 계약을 하다

We must have a contract.
Urinum kyeyak haeyahapnida. *(Uu-ree-nuhm kay-yahk hay-yah-hahp-nee-dah)* 우리는 계약해야 합니다.

Please sign this contract.
I kyehak-e somyong hashipshio. *(Ee kay-yahk-eh sah-m'yung hah-ship-she-oh)* 이 계약에 서명하십시오.

I want to cancel this contract.
Kyeyak-ul chwisohago shipsumnida. *(Kay-yahk-uhl chwee-so-hah-go ship-sume-nee-dah)* 계약을 취소하고 싶습니다.

Where do I sign?
Ssain-eul odie hajiyo? *(Sign-ruhl ah-dee-eh hah-jee-yoh?)* 싸인을 어디에 하지요?

Appointment *Yaksok* *(Yahk-soak)* 약속

Are you busy now?
Chigum pappu shimnikka? *(Chee-guhm pah-puh sheem-nee-kah?)* 지금 바쁘십니까?

I have an appointment.
Yaksog-i issumnida. *(Yahk-soag-ee ee-sume-nee-dah)* 약속이 있습니다.

How much do you charge for a consultation?
Uinon benun irhoe-e olma imnikka? *(We-non-bee-nuun er-hway-e ohlm-mah eem-nee-kah?)* 의논비는 일 회에 얼마입니까?

Are there many attorneys in Korea?
Hanguk-e nun pyonhosa duli manssumnikka?
(Hah-guuk-eh nuun pyahn-hoh-sah duh-lee mahn-sume-nee-kah?) 한국에는 변호사들이 많습니까?

Bank* *Unhaeng* (Uhn-hang) 은행

*Banking in Korea is highly automated.

ATM	*Hyon Gumji Gupki* (*Hyun Guhm-jee Guhp-kee*) 현금지급기
bank account	*kyechwa* (*kay- chwah*) 계좌
bankbook	*tongjang* (*tong-jahng*) 통장
deposit	*ipgum* (*eep-guhm*) 입금
withdraw	*chulgum* (*chul-guhm*) 출금
wire transfer	*songum* (*sohng-guhm*) 송금
balance	*janaek* (*jahn-eek*) 잔액
charge	*susuryo* (*suu-suu-ryoh*) 수수료
credit card	*shinyong kadu* (*sheen-yohng kah-duu*) 신용카드
debit card	*cheku kadu* (*check kah-duu*) 체크카드

I need to go to a bank.
Unhaeng-e kaya hamnida. (*Uhn-hang-eh kah-yah hahm-nee-dah*) 은행에 가야합니다.

What time do banks open?
Unhaeng-un myot shie yomnikka? (*Uhn-hang-uhn m'yuht-she-eh yahm-nee-kah?*) 은행은 몇시에 엽니까?

Please change these dollars into Korean currency.
I ttal-lo-rul won-eu-ru chom pakkwo chuseyo.
(*Ee dal-lah-ruhl won-yu-ruu chome pahk-way chuu-say-you*) 이 달러를 원으로 좀 바꿔주세요.

137

I would like to open an account.
Tongjangul mandulgo shippundeyo. (*Tong-jahng-uhl mahn-dul-goh ship-puun-day-yoh*) 통장을 만들고 싶은데요.

I want to deposit money.
Ipgumul hago shippundeyo. (*Eep-guhm-uhl hah-go ship-puun-day-yoh*) 입금을 하고 싶은데요.

Can I check my balance?
Janaeki olmana itchiyo? (*Jahn-eek-ee ahl-mah-nah eet-chee-yoh?*) 잔액이 얼마나 있지요?

I lost my credit card.
Shinyong kadurul ilobollyonundeyo. (*Sheen-yohng kah-duu-ruhl eel-ah-buh-lyuh-nuun-day-yoh*) 신용카드를 잃어버렸는데요.

Citizen *Shimin* (*She-meen*) 시민

Where are you from?
Odi-e seo o-shyeo sseo yo? (*Ah-dee-eh oh-shay say-oh yoh?*) 어디에서 오셨어요?

Are you a Korean citizen?
Tangshin-un Hanguk shimin imnikka? (*Tahng-sheen-uhn Hahn-guuk she-meen eem-nee-kah?*) 당신은 한국시민입니까?

Where were you born?
Kohyang-i odiseyo? (*Koh-hyahng-ee ah-dee-say-yoh?*) 고향이 어디세요?

Where do you live?
Odi saseyo? (*Ah-dee sah-say-yoh?*) 어디 사세요?

I'm American.
Chonun Miguksaram-i e yo. (Choh-nuun Me-guuk-sah-rahm-ee eh-yoh) 저는 미국 사람이에요.

Japanese	*Ilbonsaram (Eel-bone-sah- rahm)* 일본사람	
Chinese	*Chungguksaram (Chuung-guuk-sah-rahm)* 중국사람	
Australian	*Hojusaram (Hoh-juu-sah-rahm)* 호주사람	
Canadian	*Kanadasaram (Kaeh-nah-dah-sah-rahm)* 캐나다사람	
British	*Yongguksaram (Yohng-guuk-sah-rahm)* 영국 사람	

98 Country *Nara (Nah-rah)* 나라

What country are you from?
Onu nara chulshin imnika? (Oh-nuu nah-rah chuul-sheen eem-nee-kah?) 어느 나라 출신입니까?

Is Korea your native country?
Hanguk-un tangshin-e kohyang imnikka?
(Hahn-guuk-uhn tahng-sheen-eh koh-yahng eem-ne-kah?) 한국은 당신의 고향입니까?

99 Consulate *Yongsagwan (Yahng-sahg-wahn)* 영사관

Is there an American consulate here?
Yogi-e Migug-ui yongsagwan-i issumika? (Yah-ghee-eh Me-guug-we yahng-sahg-wahn-ee ee-sume-nee-kah?) 여기에 미국 영사관이 있습니까?

embassy   *taesagwan* (tay-sah-gwahn) 대사관

Please take me to the American Embassy.
Meigug Taesagwan-e kachi kapshida.
(*May-guug Tay-sah-gwahn-eh kah-chee kahp-she-dah*)
미국대사관에 같이 갑시다.

Home / House *Chip* (Cheep) 집

apartment	*ap'atu* (ah-pah-tuh) 아파트
household (family)	*kajong* (kah-johng) 가정
room	*bang* (bahng) 방
kitchen	*chubang* (chuu-bahng) 주방
living (sitting) room	*koshil* (kuu-sheel) 거실
dining room	*shi tang* (she tahng) 식당
bathroom	*yokshil* (yoke-sheel) 욕실
entrance	*hyongwan* (h'yuhn-gwahn) 현관
terrace	*beiranda* (bay-rahn-dah) 베란다
furniture	*gagu* (gah-guh) 가구
sopa	*sopa* (so-pah) 소파
bed	*chimdae* (chim-day) 침대
closet	*otjang* (ot-jahng) 옷장
drawer	*sorapjang* (suh-rahp-jahng) 서랍장
bookshelf	*chaekjang* (chack-jahng) 책장
dining table	*shiktak* (sheek-tahk) 식탁

Thank you for the invitation.
Chodaehae chusyoso kamsahamnida. (*Choh-day-hay chuu-show-suh kahm-sah-hahm-nee-dah*) 초대해 주셔서 감사합니다.

Please sit here.
Yogi anjuseyo. (Yoh-ghee ahn-ju-say-yoh) 여기 앉으세요.

This looks delicious!
Chal mokke ssumnida.* (Chahl moke-kuh sume-nee-dah)
잘 먹겠습니다.

* Literally, "I will eat well," said by the guest at the beginning of a meal.

Thank you for a wonderful meal.
Madshitnun shiksa kamsa hamnida.
(Mah-seet-nuun sheek-sah kahm-sah hahm-nee-dah)
맛있는 식사 감사합니다.

Thank you for the delicious food.
Chal mogossupnida. (Chahl moh-guh-suhm-ni-dah)
잘 먹었습니다.

I enjoyed it very much.
Chungmal maditke mogossumnida.
(Chung-mahl mah-dee-kuh moh-guh-sume-nee-dah)
정말 맛있게 먹었습니다.

Goodbye!
Annyonghi kyeseyo. (Ahn-n'yohng-he keh-say-yoh)
안녕히 계세요.

Measurements *Chisu (chee-suu)* 치수

Please take my measurements.
Chisu-rul chae chuseyo. (Chee-suu-ruhl chay chuu-say-yoh)
치수를 재주세요.

1 centimeter	[*sentimito (sen-tee-mee-tah)* 센티미터] = 0.3987 inch [*inchi (in-chee)* 인치]
30.40 centi- meters	[*sentimito (sen-tee-mee-tah)* 센티미터 = 1 foot [*puteu (pu-tuh)* 인치]
1 meter	[*mito (mee-tah)* 미터] = 3.281 feet [*piteu (pee-tuh)* 피트]
1 kilometer	[*killomito (keel-loh-mee-tah)* 킬로미터] = 0.6214 mile [*mail (mah-eel)* 마일]
1 gram	[*geuraem (guh-rahm)* 그램] = 0.03527 ounce [*ounseu (oun-suh)* 온스]
1 kilogram	[*killogeuraem (keel-loh-guh-rahm)* 킬로그램] = 2.205 pounds [*paundeu (poun-duh)* 파운드]
1 ounce	[*ounseu (oun-suh)* 온스] = 28.35 grams [*geuraem (guh-rahm)* 그램]
1 pound	[*paundeu (poun-duh)* 파운드] = 453.6 grams [*geuraem (guh-rahm)* 그램]

Personal Titles

The Korean language has many traditional forms of address
for individuals, depending on their gender, age, social class,
relationship and so on. Learning and using them correctly
is a major chore. As a result, more and more Koreans are
resorting to the use of common English titles, even when
dealing with other Koreans. The use of English titles by
foreigners is perfectly acceptable.

Mr./Mrs.	*Ssi (sshe)* 씨
also:	*Songsangnim (suung-sang-neem)* 선생님

Academic Titles

dean	*hakchang (hahk-chahng)* 학장
lecturer	*kangsa (kahng-sah)* 강사
full-time lecturer	*chonim kangsa (chuh-neem kahng-sah)* 전임강사
part-time lecturer	*shigan kangsa (she-gahn kahng-sah)* 시간강사
professor	*kyosu (k'yoe-suu)* 교수
associate professor	*bu kyosu (buu-k'yoe-suu)* 부교수
assistant professor	*cho kyosu (choh-k'yoe-suu)* 조교수
adjunct professor	*kyumim kyosu (k'yohm-eem-k'yoe-suu)* 겸임교수
emeritus professor	*myonye kyosu (m'yung-yay k'yoe-suu)* 명예교수
scholar	*hakcha (hahk-chah)* 학자
teacher	*kyosa (k'yoe-sah)* 교사

Business & Professional Titles

accountant	*hoegyesa (whey-gay-sah)*	회계사
ambassador	*taesa (day-sah)*	대사
architect	*konchukkisa (kuh-ahn-chuke-ke-sah)*	건축기사
artist	*yesulga (yay-suhl-gah)*	예술가
astronaut	*wuju pihaengsa (wuu-juu bee-hang-sah)*	우주 비행사
author	*choja (chu-jah)*	저자
athlete	*undongson-su (unn-doong-sun-suu)*	운동선수
businessman	*saopka (sah-up-kah)*	사업가
company employee	*hoesawon (hwaysahwuhn)*	회사원
company executive	*hoesa kanbu (whay-sah kahn-buu)*	회사간부
cook	*yorisa (yoh-ree-sah)*	요리사
dentist	*chikkwaeuisa (cheek-kway-we-sah)*	치과의사
diplomat	*oegyogwan (way-g'yoh-gwahn)*	외교관
doctor	*euisa (eh-wee-sah)*	의사
engineer	*kisuljja (kee-suhl-jah)*	기술자
entertainer	*yonyein (yuhn-yay-een)*	연예인
firefighter	*sobangkwan (soh-bahng-kwahn)*	소방관
government official	*gongmuwo (gong-muu-wohn)*	공무원
homemaker	*kajongjubu (kah-jung-juu-buu)*	가정주부
hairdresser	*miyongsa (me-yohng-sah)*	미용사

interpreter	*tongyoksa* (*tohng-yuk-sah*) 통역사
journalist	*shinmun chapchi kija* (*sheen-muun chahp-chee kee-jah*) 신문잡지 기자
judge	*pansa* (*pahn-sah*) 판사
lawyer	*pyonhosa* (*p'yone-hoh-sah*) 변호사
manager	*chibaein* (*chee-bay-een*) 지배인
military officer	*yukkun changgyo* (*yuke-kuun chahng-g'yoe*) 육군장교
movie director	*yonghwa kamdok* (*yohng-hwah kahm-dok*) 영화 감독
novelist/writer	*chakka* (*chack-kah*) 작가
nurse	*kanhowon* (*kahn-hoh-wan*) 간호원
office worker	*sa muwon* (*sah muu-wan*) 사무원
pharmacist	*yaksa* (*yahk-sah*) 약사
photographer	*saijin chakka* (*sigh-jeen chack-kah*) 사진 작가
pilot	*chojongsa* (*choh-johng-sah*) 조종사
politician	*chongchiga* (*chohng-chee-gah*) 정치가
police officer	*kyongchal* (*k'yung-chahl*) 경찰
private secretary	*pisu* (*bee-suu*) 비서
prosecutor	*komsa* (*kuum-sah*) 검사
public official	*kongmuwo* (*kong-muu-wohn*) 공무원
scientist	*kwahakcha* (*kwah-hahk-chah*) 과학자
singer	*kasu* (*kah-suu*) 가수
soldier	*kunin* (*kuun-een*) 군인
teacher	*kyosa* (*k'yoe-sah*) 교사; *songsangnim* (*suung-sang-neem*) 선생님
veterinarian	*sueuisa* (*suu-eh-wee-sah*) 수의사

Holidays

national holiday	*kukkyongil (kuuk-k'yohng-eel)* 국경일
vacation	*hyuil (h'yuu-eel)* 휴일
New Year's Day (January 1)	*Shin-jong Sol-lal (Sheen-johng sohl- lahl)* 신정 설날
Lunar New Year (1st lunar month, 1st day)	*Ku-jong Sol-lal (Sheen-johng sohl-lahl)* 구정 설날
Independence Day (March 1)	*Sam-il Jol (Sahn-eel Johl)* 삼일 절
Arbor Day (April 5)	*Shing-mo Gil (Sheeng-moh Geel)* 식목일
Buddha's Birthday (4th lunar month, 8th day)	*Sokgatanshinil (Suhk-gah-tahn-sheen-eel)* 석가 탄신일
Children's Day (May 5)	*Eorin-e Nal (Eh-yoh-reen-ee Nahl)* 어린이날
Memorial Day (June 6)	*Hyon-chung Il (H'yohn-chung Eel)* 현충일
Constitution Day (July 17)	*Che-hon Jeol (Chuh-hohn Johl)* 제헌절
Liberation Day (August 15)	*Kwang-bok Jol (Kwahng-boak Johl)* 광복절
Thanksgiving Day (8th lunar month, 15th day)	*Chusok (Chuu-soak)* 추석
Armed Forces Day (October 1)	*Kukukkun-eul Nal (Kuu-kuu-kkuun-yuhl Nahl)* 국군의 날
National Foundation Day (October 3)	*Kae Chon Jol (Kay Chohn Johl)* 개천절

Hangul Day (October 9)	*Hangul Lal (Hahn-guhl Lahl)* 한글날
Christmas Day (December 25)	*Song-tahn Jol (Sahng-tahn Johl)* 성탄절

Popular Destinations in Seoul

American embassy	*Miguk Taesagwan (Me-guuk Tay-sah-gwahn)* 미국 대사관
Chinese embassy	*Chungguk Taesagwan (Chuung-guuk Tay-sah-gwahn)* 중국 대사관
Japanese embassy	*Ilbon Taesagwan (Eel-bohn Tay-sah-gwahn)* 일본 대사관
East Gate	*Tong Daemun (Toong Day-muun)* 동대문
Insadong Antique Street	*Insadong koldongpum Geori (In-sa-dong kohl -dong-pum geo-ree)* 인사동 골동품거리
Itaewon Shopping District	*Itaewon Syoping Kuyok (Ee-tay-won Shope-peeng Kuh-yuk)* 이태원 쇼핑 구역
Great South Gate Market	*Nam Dae Mun Shijang (Nahm Day Muun She-jahng)* 남대문 시장
Kyongbok Palace	*Kyongbok Kung (K'yohng-bok Kuung)* 경복궁
National Central Kyongbok Palace grounds)	*Kungnip Chungang Pangmulgwan (Kuung-neep Chuun-gahng Pahng-muhl Gwahn)* 국립중앙 박물관

National Folklore Museum	*Minsok Pangmul Gwan* (*Meen-soak Pahng-muhl-gwahn*) 민속 박물관
Myungdong Shopping Disctrict	*Myungdong Syoping Kuyok* (*M'yohng-dong Shope-peeng Kuh-yuk*) 명동 쇼핑구역
Panmunjom/DMZ	*Panmunjom* (*Pahn-muun-johm*) 판문점
Pulguk Temple	*Pulguk Sa* (*Puhl-guuk Sah*) 불국사
Secret Garden	*Pi Won* (*Bee Won*) 비원
Seoul Arts Center	*Yesure Chong Dang* (*Yay-suu-ray Chong Dahng*) 예술의 전당
South Mountain Park	*Nam San Kongwon* (*Nahm Sahn Kong-wohn*) 남산 공원
South Mountain Tower	*Nam San Tawo* (*Nahm Sahn Tao-ah*) 남산 타워
Toksu Palace	*Tokusu Gung* (*Tuhk-suu Guung*) 덕수궁

PART 3

Pronunciation Guide for Key Names & Signs

The Nine Provinces

Chejudo	*(Cheh-juu-doh)* 제주도
Chollabuk-do	*(Chol-la-buuk-doh)* 전라북도
Chollanam-do	*(Chol-la-nahm-doh)* 전라남도
Ch'ungch'ongbuk-do	*(Chuung-chohng-buuk-doh)* 충청북도
Ch'ungch'ongnam-do	*(Chuung-chohng-nahm-doh)* 충청남도
Kangwon-do	*(Kahng-won-doh)* 강원도
Kyonggi-do	*(K'yohng-ghee-doh)* 경기도
Kyongsangbuk-do	*(K'yohng-sahng-buuk-doh)* 경상북도
Kyongsangnam-do	*(K'yohng-sahn-nahm-doe)* 경상남도

Major Cities

Seoul	*(So-uhl)* 서울
Pusan	*(Buu-sahn)* 부산
Taegu	*(Tay-guu)* 대구
Inch'on	*(Inn-chahn)* 인천
Kwangju	*(Kwahng-juu)* 광주
Taejon	*(Tay-joan)* 대전
Kyongju	*(K'yohng-juu)* 경주
Pohang	*(Poe-hahng)* 포항
Chunchon	*(Chune-chahn)* 춘천

Other Key Words

capital	*sudo* (*suu-doh*)	수도
city	*toshi* (*toh-she*)	도시
coast	*haean* (*hay-ahn*)	해안
East Sea	*Tong Hae* (*Doong Hay*)	동해
hill	*ondok* (*ahn-doak*)	언덕
lake	*hosu* (*hoh-suu*)	호수
mountain	*san* (*sahn*)	산
ocean	*pada* (*pah-dah*)	바다
Pacific Ocean	*Tae-p'yong Yang* (*Day P'-yohng Yahng*)	태평양
province	*to / do* (*doh*)	도
river	*kang* (*kahng*)	강
rural area	*shi gol* (*she guhl*)	시골
town	*sodoshi* (*soh-doe-she*)	소도시
village	*maeul* (*may-uhl*)	마을
Yellow Sea	*Hwang Hae* (*Hwahng Hay*)	황해

Common Signs

Knowing how to read public signs is one of the most important language assets one can have when visiting a foreign country. Here are some of the important signs you will see in Korea:

Entrance	*Ipku* (*Eep-kuu*)	입구
Push	*Milda* (*Meel-dah*)	밀다
Pull	*Dang-gi-da* (*Tah-gah-chee*)	당기다
Exit	*Chulgu* (*Chul-guu*)	출구
Emergency Exit	*Pisang Gu* (*Bee-sahng Guu*)	비상구
Toilet	*Pyongi* (*Bee-yohn-ghee*)	변기

Men	*Namja (Nahm-jah)* 남자
Women	*Yoja (Yoh-jah)* 여자
Open	*Yolda (Yohl-dah)* 열다
Closed	*Tatta (Daht-tah)* 닫다
Danger	*Wihom (Wee-huum)* 위험
No Smoking	*Kum Yon (Kuum Yohn)* 금연
Fire Alarm	*Hwajae Kyongbogi (Hwah-jay K'yohng-boh-ghee)* 화재 경보기
Fire Extinguisher	*Hwajae Sohwagi (Hwah-jay Soh-whah-ghee)* 화재 소화기
Information	*Annae So (Ahn-nay Soh)* 안내소
Cashier	*Chulnapkye (Chul-nop-kay)* 출납계
Parking Lot	*Chucha Jang (Chuu-chah Jahng)* 주차장
Hospital	*Pyongwon (B'yohng-won)* 병원

[A]

abroad (overseas)	*haeoe-e (hay-way-eh)* 해외에
accident	*sago (sah-goh)* 사고
accommodation	*suksso (suuk-soh)* 숙소
account	*kyesan (kay-sahn)* 계산
acquaintance	*anun saram (ah-nun sah-rahm)* 아는 사람
actor	*paeu (pay-uu)* 배우
acupuncture	*chimchiryo (cheem-chee-rio)* 침치료
address (location)	*chuso (chuu-soh)* 주소
admission	*ipchang (eep-chahng)* 입장
admission fee	*ipchang nyo (eep-chahng n'yoh)* 입장료
admission ticket	*ipchang kwon (eep-chahng kwun)* 입 장권
adult	*orun (uh-ruhn)* 어른
advertise	*kwanggohada (kwahng- goh-hah- dah)* 광고하다
advertisement	*kwanggo (kwahng-goh)* 광고
advice	*chunggo (chuung-goh)* 충고
adviser	*choonja (choh-unn-jah)* 조언자
afternoon	*ohu (oh-huu)* 오후
agency	*taeri (day-ree)* 대리
agent	*taeri (day-ree)* 대리
agreement (assent)	*tongui (dohng-we)* 동의
agreement (contract)	*kyeyak (kay-yahk)* 계약

agriculture	*nongop (nohn-guhp)* 농업
AIDS	*EIJI (a-e-jee)* 에이즈
airbase	*konggun kiji (kohng- guun kee-jee)* 공군 기지
air force	*konggun (kohng-guun)* 공군
airplane	*pi-hang-gi (pee-hang-ghee)* 비행기
airport	*konghang (kohng-hahng)* 공항
aisle	*tong-no (tuung-no)* 통로
alcohol	*al-kol (ah-kohl)* 알콜
alien (foreigner)	*oegugin (way-guug-een)* 외국인
allergy	*allerugi (ahl-lur-ghee)* 알레르기
alley (back street)	*kolmok (kohl-moak)* 골목
alphabet	*alp'abet (ahl-pah-bet)* 알파벳
altitude	*kodo (koh-doh)* 고도
a.m.	*ojon (oh-jahn)* 오전
ambassador	*taesa (tay-sah)* 대사
ambulance	*ku-gup-cha (kuu-guup-chah)* 구급차
America	*Miguk (Me-guuk)* 미국
American	*Miguksaram (Me-guuk-sah-rahm)* 미국사람
American embassy	*Miguk Taesagwan (Me-guuk Tay-sah-gwahn)* 미국 대사관
ancestor	*chosang (choh-sahng)* 조상
animal	*tongmul (tohng-muhl)* 동물
anniversary	*kinyohmil (keen-yuh-meel)* 기념일
announcement	*kongpyo (kohng-p'yoh)* 공표
antibiotic	*hangsang mulchil (hahng-sang muhl-cheel)* 항생물질
antique	*koldongpum (kohl-doong-puum)* 골동품
apartment	*ap'atu (ah-pah-tuh)* 아파트

apologize	**sagwahada** *(sahg-wah-hah-dah)* 사과하다
apology	**sagwa** *(sahg-wah)* 사과
appetite	**sigyok** *(she-g'yoak)* 식욕
appetizer	**an-ju** *(ahn-juu)* 안주
application	**chimang** *(chee-mahng)* 지망
appointment	**yaksok** *(yahk-sohk)* 약속
apprentice	**toje** *(toh-jay)* 도제
approval	**sungin** *(suhn-geen)* 승인
architecture	**konchuk** *(kuhn-chuuk)* 건축
arrival	**tochak** *(toh-chock)* 도착 / **ipgu** *(eep-guu)* 입국
arrival gate	**tochak mun** *(toh-chock muun)* 도착문
arrive	**tochakhada** *(toh-chock-hah-dah)* 도착하다
art	**mesul** *(mee-suhl)* 미술
art gallery	**hwa rang** *(hwah rahng)* 화랑
artist	**yesulga** *(yeh-suhl-gah)* 예술가
Asia	**Asia** *(Asia)* 아시아
Asian	**Asia saram** *(Asia sah-rahm)* 아시아 사람
aspirin	**asupirin** *(ahs-pee-reen)* 아스피린
assistant	**chosu** *(choh-suu)* 조수
association	**hyopoe** *(h'yoh-pway)* 협회
athlete	**sonsu** *(sohn-suu)* 선수
Atlantic Ocean	**Taesoyang** *(Day-suh-yahng)* 대서양
ATM	**Hyon Gumji Gupki** *(Hyun Guhm-jee Guhp-kee)* 현금지급기
audience	**chongjung** *(chohng-juhng)* 청중
auditorium	**kangdang** *(kahng-dahng)* 강당

aunt	*imo (iee-mo)* 이모
Australia	*Hoju (Hoh-juu)* 호주 / *Ostreillia (Australia)* 오스트레일리아
automobile	*chadongcha (chah-dohng-chah)* 자동차
autumn	*kaul (kah-uhl)* 가을
award	*sangpum (sahng-pume)* 상품
[B]	
baby	*aegi (aa-ghee)* 애기
babysitter	*ai tolponun saram (aye dohl-poh-nuhn sah-rahm)* 아이 돌보는 사람
backpack	*paenang (pay-nahng)* 배낭
bag	*kabang (kah-bahng)* 가방
baggage	*chim (cheem)* 짐
baggage claim	*suha mul (suu-hah muhl)* 수하물
bakery	*pangjip (pahng-jeep)* 빵집
ball	*kong (kohng)* 공
ball field	*undongjang (uun-dohng-jahng)* 운동장
bandage	*pungdae (puung-day)* 붕대
band-aid	*ilhoyongpanchang-go (eel-hoh-yohng-pahn-chahng-go)* 일회용 반창고
bank	*unhang (uun-hang)* 은행
banker	*unhangga (uun-hang-gah)* 은행가
banquet	*yonhoe (yuun-whey)* 연회
bar	*ppa (bah)* 바
barbershop	*ibalso (ee-bahl-suh)* 이발소
bargain	*hungjong (hung-juung)* 흥정
baseball	*yagu (yah-guu)* 야구
basketball	*nonggu (nohng-guu)* 농구

bath	**mogyok** *(moag-yoak)* 목욕
bath house	**mogyok tang** *(moag-yoak tahng)* 목욕탕
bathing suit	**suyong bok** *(suu-yuhng bohk)* 수영복
bathroom	**mogyokssil** *(moag-yoak-sheel)* 목욕실
batteries	**boetori** *(baa-toh-ree)* 배터리
bay	**man** *(mahn)* 만
beach	**haesuyokjiang** *(hay-suu-yoak-jee-ahng)* 해수욕장
bean curd	**tu-bu** *(tuh-buhh)* 두부
bear	**gom** *(gohm)* 곰
beautiful	**arumdaun** *(ah-ruhm-dah-uun)* 아름다운
beauty parlor	**mijang won** *(me-jahng won)* 미장원
bed	**chindae** *(cheen-day)* 침대
bedroom	**chimsil** *(cheem-sheel)* 침실
beef (broiled)	**pulgogi** *(puhl-go-ghee)* 불고기
beef ribs, broiled	**pulgalbi** *(puhl-gahl-bee)* 불갈비
beef steak	**pipusuteiku** *(be-puu-stay-kuu)* 비프스테이크
beer	**maekchu** *(make-chuu)* 맥주 / **bio** *(be-ah)* 비어
beer hall	**bio hol** *(be-ah hall)* 비어홀
bicycle	**chajongo** *(chah-johng-oh)* 자전거
bill	**kyesanso** *(kay-sahn-suh)* 계산서
bill(s), currency	**jari** *(jah-ree)* 짜리
birthday	**saengil** *(sang-eel)* 생일
black market	**amshijang** *(ahm-she-jahng)* 암시장
blanket	**tamnyo** *(dahm-n'yoh)* 담요
blond	**kumbarui** *(kuhm-bahr-we)* 금발의
blood	**pi** *(bee)* 피

blood pressure	*hyo rap (h'yuh rahp)* 혈압
boat	*pae (pay)* 배
bone	*pyo (p'yoh)* 뼈
bonus	*ponosu (boh-nah-suu)* 보너스
book	*chaek (chake)* 책
bookstore	*sojom (suh-juum)* 서점
booth (stand)	*pusu (buu-suu)* 부스
border	*kukkyong (kuuk-k'yung)* 국경
bosom	*kasum (kah-suhm)* 가슴
boss	*bosu (boh-suu)* 보스
bottle	*pyong (b'yohng)* 병
bouquet	*kkottabal (koht-tah-bahl)* 꽃다발
bowl	*sabal (sah-bahl)* 사발
box	*sangja (sahng-jah)* 상자
boyfriend	*namja chingu (nahm-jah cheen-guu)* 남자친구
branch (office)	*chijom (chee-juum)* 지점
brand	*sangpyo (sahng-p'yoh)* 상표
bread	*pang (pahng)* 빵
breakfast	*achimshiksa (ah-cheem-sheek-sah)* 아침식사 / *choban (choh-bahn)* 조반
brewery	*yangjojang (yahng-joh-jahng)* 양조장
bribe	*noemul (no-eh-muhl)* 뇌물
bride	*shinbu (sheen-buu)* 신부
bridegroom	*shillang (sheel-lahng)* 신랑
briefcase	*kabang (kah-bahng)* 가방
Britain	*Yongguk (Yohng-guuk)* 영국
British (person)	*Yongguksaram (Yohng-guuk-sah-rahm)* 영국사람

British embassy	*Yongguk Taesagwan* (*Yohng-guuk Tay-sah-gwahn*) 영국대사관
brochure	*sochaekcha* (*soh-chake-chah*) 소책자
broker	*purouko* (*buu-roh-kah*) 브로커
brothers	*hyeongjae* (*hyeong-jeh*) 형제
Buddhism	*Pulgyo* (*Puhl-g'yoh*) 불교
buddy (friend)	*chingu* (*cheen-guu*) 친구
budget	*yesan* (*yay-sahn*) 예산
buffet	*changchang* (*chahng-chang*) 부페
building	*kunmul* (*kuhn-muhl*) 건물
bus	*bosu* (*buh-suu*) 버스
bus stop	*bosu chongnyujang* (*buh-suu chong-n'yuu-jahng*) 버스 정류장
business	*yongmu* (*yohng-muu*) 용무
business hours	*yongop shigan* (*yohng-guup she-gahn*) 영업시간
businessman	*shiropka* (*she-rup-kah*) 실업가
by oneself	*honja* (*hohn-jah*) 혼자
[C]	
cab	*taekshi* (*tack-she*) 택시
cabaret	*kyabare* (*k'yah-bah-ray*) 캬바레
cable TV	*keibul tibi* (*kay-e-buul-dee-bee*) 케이블 티비
café	*kape* (*kah-pay*) 카페
cake	*keiku* (*kay-e-kuu*) 케이크
calculator	*kyesangi* (*kay-sahn-ghee*) 계산기
calendar	*tallyok* (*tahl-l'yuhk*) 달력
camera	*kamera* (*kah-may-rah*) 카메라
camera shop	*kamera kage* (*kah-may-rah kah-gay*) 카메라 가게

campus	**kaempous** (*came-pah-suu*) 캠퍼스
Canada	**Kanada** (*Kaeh-nah-dah*) 캐나다
Canadian	**Kanadasaram** (*Kaeh-na-dah-sah-rahm*) 캐나다사람
cancel	**malsarhada** (*mahl-sahr-hah-dah*) 말살하다
cancer	**am** (*ahm*) 암
candy	**kaendi** (*candy*) 캔디
capital (money)	**chabon** (*chah-bohn*) 자본
capitalism	**chabonjuui** (*chah-bohn-juu-wee*) 자본주의
car	**cha** (*chah*) 차
card (business)	**myong ham** (*m'yohng hahm*) 명함
card (playing)	**turompu** (*tuu-rahm-puu*) 트럼프
cash	**hyon-gum** (*h'yuhn-guhm*) 현금
cashier	**chulnapkye** (*chul-nahp-keh*) 출납계
catalog	**katallougu** (*kah-tahl-low-guu*) 카탈로그
cell phone	**handu pon** (*hahn-duu pohn*) 핸드폰
centimeter	**sentimito** (*sen-tee-mee-tah*) 센티미터
ceremony	**yesik** (*yay-sheek*) 예식
chair	**uija** (*we-jah*) 의자
change (coins)	**chandon** (*chahn-dohn*) 잔돈
charge (price wanted)	**chaegim** (*chay-geem*) 책임
charming	**maeryokchogin** (*mayer-ryuk-cho-geen*) 매력적인
chauffeur	**unjonkisa** (*uun-joan-kee-sah*) 운전기사
check (bill)	**kyesanso** (*kay-sahn-soh*) 계산서
check (money)	**supyo** (*suup-yoh*) 수표

check-in (at airport)	***tapsung susok*** *(tahp-suung suu-soak)* 탑승 수속
child / children	***ai*** *(aye)* 아이 / ***aidul*** *(aye-duhl)* 아이들
China	***Chunggong*** *(Chuung-gohng)* 중국
Chinese language	***Chunggu-mal*** *(Chuung-guu mahl)* 중국말
Chinese person	***Chungguk saram*** *(Chuung-guuk sah-rahm)* 중국 사람
chocolate	***chokalet*** *(choh-kah-let)* 쵸코렛
chopsticks	***chokkarak*** *(chuh-kah-rahk)* 젓가락
church	***kyohoe*** *(k'yoh-whey)* 교회
citizen	***shimin*** *(she-meen)* 시민
citizenship	***shiminkwon*** *(she-meen-kwun)* 시민권
claim	***yogu*** *(yoh-guu)* 요구
classroom	***kyosil*** *(kyuh-sheel)* 교실
clean	***kkekkuthan****(kuh-kuh-hanh)* 깨끗한
climate	***kihu*** *(kee-huu)* 기후
clock / watch	***shigye*** *(she-gay)* 시계
coffee shop	***kopi shop*** *(koh-pee shop)* 커피숍
coke (Coca-cola)	***kokakolla*** *(koh-kah-koh-lah)* 코카콜라
comb	***moribit*** *(moh-ree-beet)* 머리빗
compact disc	***kompaktu disuku*** *(kome-pahk-tuu-dees-kuu)* 컴팩트 디스크
company	***hoesa*** *(hwey-sah)* 회사
competitor	***kyongjengja*** *(k'yohng-jang-jah)* 경쟁자
complaint	***pulpyong*** *(puhl-pyung)* 불평
computer	***kompyuto*** *(kome-pyu-tah)* 컴퓨터
concert	***umakoe*** *(uh-mah-koh-eh)* 음악회

condom	**kondom** *(condom)* 콘돔
conference	**hoeui** *(hwey-we)* 회의
confirmation	**hwaginso** *(hwah-geen-soh)* 확인서
Confucius	**Kongja** *(Kohng-jah)* 공자
consulate	**yongsagwan** *(yuhng-sah-gwahn)* 영사관
contact lens	**kontaktu renjo** *(kohn-tack-tuu ren-ju)* 콘텍트 렌즈
convenient store	**pyonuijom** *(pyahn-wee-jome)* 편의점
cook (verb)	**yori** *(yoh-ree)* 요리
cook (noun)	**yorisa** *(yoh-ree-sah)* 요리사
cookie	**kwaja** *(kwah-jah)* 과자
copier	**poksagi** *(poke-sah-gee)* 복사기
cosmetic	**hwajangpum** *(hwah-jahng-puhm)* 화장품
couple	**ssang** *(ssang)* 쌍
course	**suop** *(suu-up)* 수업
cousin	**sachon** *(sah- chuhn)* 사촌
cover charge	**ipjiang nyo** *(eep-jee-ahng n'yoh)* 입장료
cow	**so** *(soh)* 소
crab	**ke** *(kay)* 게
credit card	**kuridit kadu** *(kuu-re-deet kah-duh)* 크레디트 카드 / **shinyong kadu** *(sheen-yohng kah-duu)* 신용 카드
currency (Korean)	**won** *(won)* 원
currency exchange	**hwan jon** *(wahn jahn)* 환전
customer	**sonnim** *(soan-neem)* 손님
cute	**kwiyoun** *(kwee-yuh-uun)* 귀여운

[D]

dad	*appa* (*ahp-pah*) 아빠
daily	*maeil* (*may-eel*) 매일
damage	*sonhae* (*sohn-hay*) 손해
dangerous	*wihomhan* (*we-huhm-hahn*) 위험한
date (calendar)	*naljia* (*nahl-jah*) 날짜
date (romantic)	*teitu* (*day-tuu*) 데이트
date of birth	*saeng il* (*sang eel*) 생일
daughter	*dal* (*dahl*) 딸
debit card	*hyon Gum kadu* (*hyun Guhm kah-duu*) 현금 카드 / *jigbul kadu* (*jeeg-buhl kah-duu*) 직불 카드
delivery	*paedal* (*pay-dahl*) 배달
department store	*paek wajom* (*pake wah-jum*) 백화점
departure	*chubal* (*chuu-bahl*) 출발
deposit	*ipgum* (*eep-guhm*) 입금
design	*solgye* (*suhl-geh*) 설계
desk	*chaeksang* (*chake-shang*) 책상
dessert	*husik* (*huu-sheek*) 후식 / *tijotu* (*dee-jah-tuu*) 디저트
destination	*mokchokchi* (*moke-chuk-chee*) 목적지
diabetes	*tangnyobyong* (*tahng-n'yoh-byung*) 당뇨병
dialect	*saturi* (*sah-tuu-ree*) 사투리
diarrhea	*solsa* (*suhl-sah*) 설사
dictionary	*sojon* (*soh-juhn*) 사전
difficult	*oryoun* (*uh-rio-unn*) 어려운
dining	*siksa* (*sheek-sah*) 식사

dining car	*sikttangcha (sheek-dahng-chah)* 식당차
dining room	*sikttang (sheek-dahng)* 식당
dinner	*chonyok (chun-yuhk)* 저녁
discount	*harin (hah-reen)* 할인
dish	*kurut(kuu-ruht)* 그릇
display (show)	*chonsihada (chune-she-hah-dah)* 전시하다
divorced	*ihonhan (ee-hohn-hahn)* 이혼한
DMZ (De-Militarized Zone)	*Pimujang Jidae (Pee-muu-jahng Jee day)* 비무장 지대
document	*munso (muun-suh)* 문서
domestic flight	*kuknaeson (kuuk-nay-sahn)* 국내선
door, gate	*mun (muun)* 문
dormitory	*kisuksa (kee-suhk-sah)* 기숙사
downtown city center	*jungshimga (jung-sheem-gah)* 중심가 *shinae (she-nay)* 시내
draft beer	*saeng maekchu (sang make-juu)* 생맥주
dress (Western)	*duresu (du-res-suu)* 드레스
dress (Korean)	*hanbok (hahn-boak)* 한복
driver	*unjonsu (un-joan-sah)* 운전수
driver's license	*unjon myonhojung (uhn-joan m'yohn-hoh-juung)* 운전 면허증
drugs	*mayak (mah-yahk)* 마약
drugstore	*yakkuk (yahk-kuuk)* 약국
dry cleaning	*durai kulining (duu-rye kuu-lee-neeng)* 드라이 크리닝
duty	*uimu (we-muu)* 의무
duty-free shop	*myon-se jom (m'yone-say-juhm)* 면세점

[E]

ear	*kwi (kwee)* 귀
early	*irun (ee-ruhn)* 이른
early morning	*irun achim (ee-ruhn ah-cheem)* 이른 아침
earrings	*kwigori (kwee-go-ree)* 귀고리
earth	*chigu (chee-guu)* 지구
earthquake	*chijin (chee-jeen)* 지진
eat out	*oeshik hagi (way-sheek hah-ghee)* 외식 하기
economy	*kyongje (k'yung-jay)* 경제
education	*kyoyuk (k'yoh-yuk)* 교육
eggs	*kyeran (kay-rahn)* 계란
electrical appliance	*kajon chepum (kah-joan cheh-puum)* 가전 제품
electricity	*chongi (chun-ghee)* 전기
elevator	*ellibeiteo (el-ee-bay-tor)* 엘리베이터
embassy	*taesagwan (tay-sah-gwahn)* 대사관
emergency	*wigup (we-guhp)* 위급
employee	*pigoyong-in (pee-go-yohng-een)* 피고용인
employer	*koyongju (koh-yohng-juu)* 고용주
engagement	*yakon (yah-kohn)* 약혼
engine	*enjin (in-jeen)* 엔진
England	*Yongguk (Yohng-guuk)* 영국
English language	*Yong o (Yohng oh)* 영어
entertainment (as in treat)	*chopttae (chup-day)* 접대
entrance	*iptchang (eep-chahng)* 입장
envelope	*bongtu (bang-tuu)* 봉투

escalator	*esukolleito (es-ku-lay-tor)* 에스컬레이터
etiquette	*etiket (etiquette)* 에티켓
Europe	*Yurop (Yuu-ruhp)* 유럽
European (person)	*Yuropsaram (Yuu-ruhp-sah-ram)* 유럽사람
evening	*pam (bahm)* 밤
evidence	*chunggo (chuhng-guh)* 증거
examination (test)	*sihom (she-huum)* 시험
exchange	*pakuda (pahk-kuu-dah)* 바꾸다
exchange rate	*hwan yul (hwahn yuhl)* 환율
exercise	*undong (uhn-dong)* 운동
exhibition	*chonshihoe (chun-she-whey)* 전시하다
exit	*chulgu (chuhl-guu)* 출구
expensive	*pissan (bee-sahn)* 비싼
export (verb)	*suchulhada (suu-chuhl-hah-dah)* 수출하다
eye	*nun (nuun)* 눈
[F]	
face	*eolgul (ahl-guhl)* 얼굴
factory	*kongjang (kohn-jahng)* 공장
fake	*katcha (kaht-chah)* 가짜
fall	*kaul (kah-uhl)* 가을
family	*kajok (kah-joak)* 가족
family-run bed-and- breakfast type facilities	*minbak (meen-bahk)* 민박
fan (hand held)	*puchae (puu-chay)* 부채
fan (electric)	*sonpunggi (sahn-puhng-ghee)* 선풍기

fare	*yogum* *(yoh-guum)* 요금
father	*aboji* *(ah-boh-jee)* 아버지
favorite place (to shop, etc)	*tan gol* *(than gohl)* 단골
fax	*paeksu* *(pake-suu)* 팩스
fee	*yogum* *(yoh-guum)* 요금
female	*yoja* *(yoh-jah)* 여자
ferry	*peri* *(bay-ree)* 페리
festival	*chukche* *(chuuk-chuh)* 축제
film (camera)	*pillum* *(pee-luum)* 필름
fingernail	*sontop* *(sohn-tohp)* 손톱
fire (conflagration)	*hwajae* *(hwah-jay)* 화재
fireworks	*pulkkonnori* *(puhl-kohn-no-ree)* 불꽃놀이
first (in order)	*chot* *(choat)* 첫
first-aid kit	*kugup sangja* *(kuu-guhp sahng-jah)* 구급 상자
first-class seat	*il-dung sok* *(eel-duhng suhk)* 일등석
fish (alive)	*mulgogi* *(muhl-goh-gee)* 물고기 / *sangsun* *(saeng-suhn)* 생선
fixed price	*chong ga* *(chohng gah)* 정가
flag (national)	*kukki* *(kuuk-kee)* 국가
flashlight	*pullaeshi* *(puhl-lie-she)* 플래쉬
flight (air)	*pihaeng* *(bee-hang)* 비행
flood	*hongsu* *(hohng-suu)* 홍수
floor (of building)	*chung* *(chuhng)* 층
flower	*kot* *(kaht)* 꽃
folk art	*minsok yesul* *(meen-soak yay-suhl)* 민속 예술
folk songs	*taejung gayo* *(tay-juung gah-yoh)* 대중 가요

food	**umshik** *(uum-sheek)* 음식
food (Korean)	**Hanshik** *(Hahn-sheek)* 한식
food (Western)	**Yangshik** *(Yahng-sheek)* 양식
foot	**pal** *(bahl)* 발
football (American)	**Mishik chukku** *(Me-sheek chuke-kuu)* 미식축구
football (soccer)	**chuuku** *(chuuk-kuu)* 축구
forehead	**ima** *(ee-mah)* 이마
foreign	**woguk** *(woh-guuk)* 외국
foreigner	**woguksaram** *(woh-guuk-sah-rahm)* 외국사람
forest	**samnim** *(sahm-neem)* 삼림
France	**Purangsu** *(Puu-rahng-suu)* 프랑스
free (no charge)	**muryo** *(muu-rio)* 무료
free parking	**muryo chucha** *(muu-rio chuu-chah)* 무료 주차
friend	**chingu** *(cheen-guu)* 친구
fruit	**kwail** *(kwah-eel)* 과일
full	**kadukchan** *(kah-duhk-chahn)* 가득찬
furnace	**hwaro** *(whah-roh)* 화로
furniture	**kagu** *(kah-guu)* 가구
future	**mirae** *(me-ray)* 미래
[G]	
gamble	**tobak** *(toh-bahk)* 도박
game (event)	**kyonggi** *(k'yohng-ghee)* 경기
garage	**chago** *(chah-go)* 차고
garden	**chongwon** *(chohng-won)* 정원
gas	**gasu** *(gah-suu)* 가스
gasoline	**gasollin** *(gah-so-leen)* 가솔린
gas station	**chuyu so** *(chuu-yuu soh)* 주유소
gate	**mun** *(muhn)* 문

gentleman	*sinsa (sheen-sah)* 신사
German (person)	*Togilsaram (Doh-geel-sah-ram)* 독일사람
Germany	*Togil (Doh-geel)* 독일
gift	*sonmul (sohn-muhl)* 선물
gift shop	*sonmul kage (sohn-muhl kah-gay)* 선물 가게
ginseng	*insam (en-sahm)* 인삼
girl	*sonyo (sohn-yuh)* 손녀
girlfriend	*yoja chingu (yuh-jah cheen-guu)* 여자친구
glasses (eye)	*angyong (ahn-g'yohng)* 안경
gloves	*changgap (chahng-gahp)* 장갑
gold	*kum (kuhm)* 금
golf	*kolpu (gohl-puu)* 골프
government	*chongbu (chohng-buu)* 정부
governor	*chisa (chee-sah)* 지사
gram	*guraem (gu-rahm)* 그램
grandfather	*haraboji (hah-rah-buh-jee)* 할아버지
grandmother	*halmoni (hahl-muh-nee)* 할머니
grocery store	*shyupomaket (shuu-pah-mah-ket)* 슈퍼마켓
groom	*shillang (sheel-lahng)* 신랑
guest	*sonnim (sohn-neem)* 손님
guide (person)	*kaidu (guy-duu)* 가이드
guidebook	*kaidubuk (guy-duu buuk)* 가이드북
gym (health club)	*helsu jang (hel-suu jahng)* 헬스장
gymnasium	*cheyukkwan (chay-yuuk-kwahn)* 체육관

[H]

hair	*mori (muh-ree)* 머리
haircut	*heokotu (hay-ah-kah-tuu)* 헤어커트
hairdresser	*ibalssa (ee-bahl-sah)* 이발사
handbag	*kabang (kah-bahng)* 가방
handicrafts	*sugongyepum (suu-gohn-gay-puum)* 수공예품
handkerchief	*sonsugun (sohn-suu-guhn)* 손수건
handmade	*sujepum (suu-jay-puum)* 수제품
harbor	*hanggu (hahng-guu)* 항구
hardware (computer)	*haduweo (hah-duu-way-ah)* 하드웨어
hat	*moja (moh-jah)* 모자
head	*mori (muh-ree)* 머리
headache	*tutong (duu-dohng)* 두통
health	*kongang (kohn-gahng)* 건강
hear	*turoyo (tuh-ruh-yoh)* 들어요
hearing aid	*pochonggi (poh-chung-ghee)* 보청기
heart	*shimjang (sheem-jahng)* 심장
heater	*hiteo (he-tah)* 히터
highway	*kosoktoro (koe-soak-doe-roe)* 고속도로
hill	*ondok (uhn-duk)* 언덕
history	*yoksa (yuk-sah)* 역사
hobby	*chwimi (ch'we-me)* 취미
hockey (ice)	*aisu haki (aye-suu hah-kee)* 아이스 하키
holiday	*hyuil (h'yuu-eel)* 휴일
public holiday	*kong hyuil (kohng h'yuu-eel)* 공휴일
hometown	*kohyang (koh-yahng)* 고향
homework	*sukje (suuk-jay)* 숙제

honey	**gul** (*guhl*) 꿀
honeymoon	**shinhon yohaeng** (*sheen-hoan yuh-hang*) 신혼 여행
Hong Kong	**Hong Kong** (*Hong Kong*) 홍콩
hospital	**pyongwon** (*p'yohng-won*) 병원
private hospital	**kaein pyongwon** (*kay-een p'yohng-won*) 개인병원
hot (to touch)	**dugoun** (*duu-gah-uun*) 뜨거운
hotel	**hot'el** (*hotel*) 호텔
hot springs	**on chon** (*uhn juhn*) 온천
hot weather	**toun** (*tuh-uun*) 더운
hour	**shigan** (*she-gahn*) 시간
house	**chip** (*cheep*) 집
housewife	**chubu** (*chuu-buu*) 주부
humid	**supkiitta** (*suup-keet-chan*) 습기찬
husband	**nampyon** (*nahm-p'yohn*) 남편
hydrofoil	**sujungiksun** (*su-jung-ik-suu*) 수중익선

[I]

ice	**orum** (*ah-ruum*) 얼음
ice cream	**aisu kurim** (*aye-suu kuu-reem*) 아이스크림
ID	**shinbunjung** (*sheen-buhn-juung*) 신분증
ill (sick)	**apun** (*ah-poon*) 아픈
illegal	**pulppopui** (*puhl-puhp-wee*) 불법의
income	**suip** (*suu-eep*) 수입
industry	**sanop** (*sah-nuhp*) 산업
infant	**aegi** (*aa-ghee*) 애기
information desk	**annae so** (*ahn-nay soh*) 안내소
injury	**pusang** (*puu-sahng*) 부상

inn (Korean)	***yogwan*** *(yuh-gwahn)* 여관
insurance	***pohom*** *(poh-hoam)* 보험
international flight	***kukjeson*** *(kuuk-jay-sahn)* 국제선
Internet café/ cybercafé	***intonet kape*** *(in-tah-net kah-pay)* 인터넷 카페
interpreter	***bongyokkwan*** *(buung-yoke-kwahn)* 번역관
intersection	***negori*** *(nay-guh-ree)* 네거리
introduction	***sogae*** *(soh-gay)* 소개
island	***som*** *(sohm)* 섬
itinerary	***yojong*** *(yuh-johng)* 여정
[J]	
jacket	***chaket*** *(chah-ket)* 자켓
Japan	***Ilbon*** *(Eel-bone)* 일본
Japanese (language)	***Ilbon o*** *(Eel-bone oh)* 일본어
Japanese (person)	***Ilbonsaram*** *(Eel-bone-sah-rahm)* 일본사람
jazz	***jaju*** *(jah-juu)* 재즈
jeans	***chongbaji*** *(chohng-bah-jee)* 청바지
jewelry	***posok*** *(boh-suk)* 보석
job	***chigop*** *(chee-guhp)* 직업
jogging	***choging*** *(jah-geen)* 조깅
journalist	***kija*** *(kee-jah)* 기자
journey	***yohaeng*** *(yu-hang)* 여행
judo	***yudo*** *(yuu-doh)* 유도
juice	***jusu*** *(juu-suu)* 주스
[K]	
karaoke	***noraebang*** *(noh-ray-bang)* 노래방

karaoke bar	*karaoke ba* (kah-rah-oh-kay bah) 카라오케 바
karate	*karade* (kah-rah-day) 카라데
key	*yolso* (yohl-soh) 열쇠
kilogram	*killoguraem* (keel-loh-gu-rahm) 킬로그램
kilometer	*killomito* (keel-loh-me-tah) 킬로미터
kisaeng (female entertainer)	*kisaeng* (kee-sang) 기생
kitchen	*chubang* (chuu-bahng) 추방
knife	*naipu* (nie-puu) 나이프 / *kal* (kahl) 칼
Korea	*Hanguk* (Hahn-guuk) 한국
Korean (language)	*Hangug o* (Hahn-guug oh) 한국어
Korean (person)	*Hanguksaram* (Hahn-guuk-sah-rahm) 한국사람
Korean studies	*Hangukhak* (Hahn-guuk-hahk) 한국학

[L]

lacquer ware	*najon chilgi* (nah-joan cheel-ghee) 나전 칠기
laundry (clothes)	*setangmul* (say-tahng-muhl) 세탁물
laundry machine	*setakgi* (say-tahk-ghee) 세탁기
law	*pop* (puhp) 법
leather	*kajuk* (kah-juke) 가죽
lecture	*kangui* (kahng-we) 강의
leisure	*yoga* (yuh-gah) 여가
lemonade	*remoneidu* (remon-a-duu) 레모네이드
letter (written)	*pyonji* (p'yohn-jee) 편지

library	**tosogwan** (*toh-suh-gwahn*) 도서관
license	**hoga** (*huh-gah*) 허가
lifeguard	**inmyongkujowon** (*een-m'yohng-kuu-joh-won*) 인명구조원
light (electric)	**pul** (*puhl*) 불
liquor	**alkool umnyo** (*alh-kah-ohl uum'nyoh*) 알콜 음료
little (amount)	**chogum** (*choh-guhm*) 조금
little (size)	**chagum** (*chah-guhm*) 작은
local bus	**maul bosu** (*mahl bah-suu*) 마을버스
lock	**chamulsoe** (*chah-muhl-swey*) 자물쇠
locker	**rok'o** (*rah-kah*) 락커
lost	**irun** (*ee-ruhn*) 잃은
lost-and-found office	**pun-shil-mul chwigup so** (*puun-sheel-muhl chwee-guup soh*) 분실물 취급소
luck	**un** (*uhn*) 운
luggage	**chim** (*cheem*) 짐
luggage locker	**chim pogwanso** (*cheem pohg-wahn-soh*) 짐 보관소
lunch	**chomshim** (*chum-sheem*) 점심
luxurious	**sachisuron** (*sah-chee-suh-ruhn*) 사치스런
luxury	**sachi** (*sah-chee*) 사치
[M]	
machine	**kigye** (*kee-gay*) 기계
made-in-country (Korea)	**kuksam pum** (*kuuk-sahm pume*) 국산품
maid	**hanyo** (*hah-yoh*) 하녀
magazine	**chapji** (*chahp-jee*) 잡지 / **chapchi** (*chahp-chee*) 잡지

mail	*pyonji* (*p'yun-jee*) 편지
mailbox	*uchetong* (*uh-chay-tong*) 우체통
major	*chunkong* (*chuhn-kohng*) 전공
manager	*chibaein* (*chee-bay-een*) 지배인 / *maenijo* (*may-nee-jah*) 매니저
map	*chido* (*chee-duh*) 지도
city map	*shinae chido* (*she-nay jee-duh*) 시내 지도
road map	*toro chido* (*doh-roh jee-duh*) 도로 지도
market (open air)	*shijang* (*she-jahng*) 시장
married	*kyoron han* (*k'yuh-rone hahn*) 결혼한
martial arts	*musul* (*muu-suhl*) 무술
martial arts (Korean)	*taekkwondo* (*tay-kwahn-doh*) 태권도
massage	*anma* (*ahn-mah*) 안마
math	*suhak* (*suu-hahk*) 수학
matinee	*natkongyon* (*naht-kohng-yohn*) 낮공연
measure	*chaeda* (*chay-dah*) 재다
medical insurance	*uiryobohom* (*we-ruh-boh-hum*) 의료보험
medicine	*yak* (*yahk*) 약
meeting	*hohap* (*hwah-hahp*) 회합
menu	*menyu* (*meh-nyuu*) 메뉴
message	*meshiji* (*may-she-jee*) 메세지
microwave	*chunjaraeingi* (*chuhn-jah-ray-inn-gee*) 전자레인지
military	*kun* (*kuun*) 군

military service	**kunbong mu** *(kuun-bohng-muu)* 군복무
mineral water	**saengsu** *(sang-suu)* 생수
minister	**moksanim** *(moke-sah-neem)* 목사님
minute	**pun** *(poon)* 분
mirror	**koul** *(koh-uul)* 거울
mistake	**shilsu** *(sheel-suu)* 실수
mobile phone	**haendu pon** *(hane-duu pohn)* 핸드폰
model (fashion)	**ponttuda** *(pohn-duu-dah)* 본뜨다
modern	**hyondaeui** *(hyun-day-wee)* 현대의
modern style	**sinsikui** *(sheen-sheek-wee)* 신식의
money	**ton** *(tone)* 돈
monk	**chung** *(chuung)* / **sunim** *(suh-neem)* 중/스님
monsoon	**changma** *(chahng-mah)* 장마
mood, feelings	**kibun** *(kee-boon)* 기분
moon	**dal** *(dahl)* 달
morning	**ojon** *(oh-jahn)* 오전
mosquito	**mogi** *(moh-ghee)* 모기
motel	**motel** *(moh-tel)* 모텔
mother	**omoni** *(uh-muh-nee)* 어머니
mother-in-law	**shiomoni** *(she-uh-muh-nee)* 시어머니
motorcycle	**otobai** *(ah-toh-by)* 오토바이
mountain	**san** *(sahn)* 산
movie	**yonghwa** *(yohng-hwah)* 영화
Mr., Mrs., Miss	**sshi** *(sshe)* 씨
museum	**pangmulgwan** *(pahng-muhl-wahn)* 박물관
music	**umak** *(uh-mahk)* 음악

musical	*myujikal* *(m'yuu-jee-kal)* 뮤지컬
[N]	
name	*irum* *(ee-ruhm)* 이름
napkin	*napkin* *(nahp-keen)* 냅킨
nation (state)	*kukka* *(kuuk-kah)* 국가
national	*kukka-e* *(kuuk-kah-eh)* 국가의
national holiday	*kukkyong il* *(kuuk-k'yuhng eel)* 국경일
nationality	*kukchok* *(kuuk-chuk)* 국적
national park	*kungnipkong won* *(kuung-neep-kohng won)* 국립공원
nature	*chayon* *(chah-yohn)* 자연
newspaper	*shinmun* *(sheen-muun)* 신문
New Year's Day	*Sol Lal* *(Sohl Lahl)* 설날
night	*yagan* *(yah-gahn)* 야간
nightclub	*naitukullop* *(nie-toh-kuu-lahb)* 나이트클럽
noise	*soum* *(soh-uhm)* 소음
non-stop flight	*jighang* *(jeeg-hahng)* 직항
noodles	*kuksu* *(kuuk-suh)* 국수
noon	*chong-o* *(chung-oh)* 정오
north	*puktchok* *(puuk-choke)* 북쪽
North Korea	*Pukan* *(Puuk-ahn)* 북한
novel	*sosol* *(soh-suhl)* 소설
number	*suryang* *(suu-r'yahng)* 수량
nurse	*kanhosa* *(kahn-hoh-sah)* 간호사
[O]	
occupation	*chigop* *(chee-gahp)* 직업
ocean	*haeyang* *(hay-yahng)* 해양
o'clock	*shi* *(she)* 시
office	*samushil* *(sah-muu-sheel)* 사무실

office worker	*samu won (sah-muu won)* 사무원
official (government)	*kwanri (kwahn-ree)* 관리
oil (automobile)	*oil (oh-eel)* 오일
ointment	*yongo (yuhn-go)* 연고
one-way ticket	*pyondo pyo (p'yohn-doh)* 편도표
open for business	*yong-opchung (yuhng uhp-chung)* 영업중
operator	*kyohwanwon (k'yoh-hwahn-won)* 교환원
opportunity	*kihoe (kee-whey)* 기회
opposite	*pandae (pahn-day)* 반대
outline	*yungwak (yuhn-gwahk)* 윤곽
overcoat	*obokotu (oh-bah-koh-tuu)* 오버코트
oyster	*kul (kuhl)* 굴
[P]	
pacemaker	*peisumeiko (pay-suu-may-kah)* 페이스메이커
Pacific Ocean	*Taepyong Yang (Day-p'yuhng Yahng)* 태평양
package	*chim (cheem)* 짐
pain	*kotong (koh-dong)* 고통
palace	*gung (guung)* 궁
paper	*chongi (chohng-ee)* 종이
parcel	*sopo (sope-oh)* 소포
parents	*pumonim (puu-moh-neem)* 부모님
park	*kongwon (kohng-won)* 공원
parking lot	*chucha jang (chuu-chah jahng)* 주차장
passenger	*sunggaek (suhng-gake)* 승객
passport	*yokwon (yoh-kwahn)* 여권

payment	*chibul (chee-buhl)* 지불
pearls	*chinju (cheen-juu)* 진주
pen	*pen (pen)* 펜
penicillin	*penishillin (pen-e-sheel-leen)* 페니실린
people	*saram-dul (sah-rahm-duhl)* 사람들
perfume	*hyangsu (hyahng-suu)* 향수
permission	*hoga (huh-gah)* 허가
pharmacy	*yakkuk (yahk-kuuk)* 약국
pickpocket	*somaechigi (soh-may-chee-ghee)* 소매치기
picture postcard	*kurim yopso (kuu-reem yup-suh)* 그림 엽서
pill	*allyak (ahl-yahk)* 알약
place	*changso (chang-soh)* 장소
planet	*yusong (yuu-suhng)* 유성
platform (train)	*pullatpom (plat-pome)* 플랫폼
p.m.	*ohu (oh-huu)* 오후
police officer	*kyongchal (k'yung-chahl)* 경찰
politician	*chongchiga (chuhng-chee-gah)* 정치가
popular music	*pap song (pahp song)* 팝송
population	*ingu (een-guu)* 인구
port	*hanggu (hahng-guu)* 항구
postcard	*upyonyopso (uup-yohn-yup-suh)* 우편엽서
post office	*ucheguk (uu-chay-guuk)* 우체국
potable water	*shik su (sheek suu)* 식수
pregnant (with child)	*imsinhan (eem-sheen-hahn)* 임신한

prepaid electronic transit pass	**kyotong kadu** (*k'yoh-tong kah-duu*) 교통카드
prescription	**chobang** (*choh-bahng*) 처방
president (of company)	**sajang** (*sah-jahng*) 사장
president (of nation)	**taetongnyong** (*day-dohng-n'yohng*) 대통령
press (media)	**sinmun** (*sheen-muun*) 신문
price	**kap** (*kahp*) 값
priest	**shinbu** (*sheen-buu*) 신부
printing	**inswae** (*een-sway*) 인쇄
private	**satchogin** (*saht-chuh-geen*) 사적인
private room	**pyol shil** (*p'yohl sheel*) 별실
profession	**chigop** (*chee-gup*) 직업
professional	**chigobui** (*chee-gub-wee*) 직업의
profit	**iik** (*eeek*) 이익
program	**puroguraem** (*puu-roh-guu-ram*) 프로그램
project	**kyehoek** (*kay-hoak*) 계획
province	**to/do** (*doh*) 도
public transportation	**taejung kyotong** (*tay-juung k'yoh-tohng*) 대중 교통
puncture	**pongku** (*pung-kuu*) 펑크
push	**miroyo** (*me-ru-yoh*) 밀어요
[Q]	
qualifications	**chagyok** (*choh-gyuhk*) 자격
quality	**tuksong** (*duuk-sohng*) 특성
quantity	**yang** (*yahng*) 양
quarantine	**kyongni** (*k'yuhng-nee*) 격리
question	**chilmun** (*cheel-muun*) 질문

quiet	*chojonghan* (*choh-johng-hahn*) 조용한
quit (give up)	*kumanduda* (*kuh-mahn-duu-dah*) 그만두다

[R]

race (breed)	*injong* (*en-johng*) 인종
radio	*radio* (*rah-dee-oh*) 라디오
railroad	*choldo* (*chohl-doh*) 철도
railway station	*kicha yok* (*kee-chah yuhk*) 기차역
rain	*pi* (*pee*) 비
raincoat	*reinkotu* (*rain-koh-tuu*) 레인코트
rainy season	*changma chol* (*chahng-mah chohl*) 장마철
rank	*chiwi* (*chee-we*) 지위
rash (skin)	*pahchin* (*pahl-cheen*) 발진
raw (uncooked)	*nalgosui* (*nahl-guh-swee*) 날것의
raw fish	*nal-saeng-suhn* (*nahl-saeng-sang*) 날생선
receipt	*yongsujung* (*yahng-suu-jahng*) 영수증
refrigerator	*naengjanggo* (*nayng-jahng-go*) 냉장고
refund	*hwanbul* (*hwahn-buhl*) 환불
region	*chibang* (*chee-bahng*) 지방
registered mail	*tunggi upyon* (*tuhng-ghee uu-p'yun*) 등기 우편
relative (kin)	*chinchok* (*cheen-choak*) 친척
religion	*chonggyo* (*chohng-g'yoh*) 종교
rent	*pilda* (*peel-dah*) 빌다
repair shop	*chong biso* (*chohng bee-soh*) 정비소
reservation	*yeyak* (*yay-yahk*) 예약

reserved seat	*chijong sok (chee-johng suk)* 지정석
rest	*hushik (huu-sheek)* 휴식
restaurant	*shiktang (sheek-tahng)* 식당
restroom	*hwajang shil (hwah-jahng sheel)* 화장실
rice (cooked)	*pap (pahp)* 밥
rice wine	*chong jong (chohng johng)* 정종
rich (wealthy)	*tonmanhun (dohn-mahn-huhn)* 돈많은
ring (for finger)	*panji (pahn-jee)* 반지
river	*kang (kahng)* 강
road	*toro (doh-roh)* 도로
romance	*aejong (aa-johng)* 애정
room	*pang (pahng)* 방
room service	*rum sobisu (rume sah-bee-suu)* 룸 서비스
round-trip ticket	*wanbok pyo (wahn-boak p'yoh)* 왕복표
rush hour	*roshiawo (rah-she-ah-wah)* 러시아워
Russia	*Roshia (Ruh-she-ah)* 러시아
[S]	
safe (for valuables)	*kumgo (kuum-go)* 금고
salary	*ponggup (pohng-guhp)* 봉급
sandwich	*sanduwichi (sand-we-chee)* 샌드위치
sanitary napkins	*saeng nidae (sang nee-day)* 생리대
sauna	*sauna (sow-nah)* 사우나
schedule	*siganpyo (she-gahn-p'yoh)* 시간표
school	*hakkkyo (hahk-k'yoh)* 학교
science	*kwahak (kwah-hahk)* 과학

scissors	**kawi** (kah-we) 가위
scrambled eggs	**pokkun dalgyal** (poke-kuhn dahl-g'yahl) 볶은 달걀
seafood	**hoemul** (hway-muhl) 해물
seashore	**hae-byon** (hie-b'yohn) 해변
seasons	**kyejol** (keh-juhl) 계절
seatbelt	**anjon beltu** (ahn-jun bel-tuu) 안전 벨트
seaweed (toasted)	**kim** (keem) 김
second-class seat	**i-dung sok** (ee-duhng suhk) 이등석
self-service	**selpu sobisu** (selp-uusah-bee-suu) 셀프서비스
semester	**hakgi** (hahk-gee) 학기
service (help)	**sobisu** (sah-bee-suu) 서비스
service charge	**sobisu ryo** (sah-be-suu rio) 서비스료
ship	**pae** (pay) 배
shirt	**shochu** (shah-chuh) 셔츠
shoeshine	**kududakki** (kuu-duu-dahk-kee) 구두닦이
shop (place)	**kage** (kah-gay) 가게
shopping	**shop'ing** (shop-eeng) 쇼핑
shopping arcade	**shop'ing akeidu** (shop-eeng ah-kay-ee-doh) 쇼핑 아케이드
shower	**shawo** (shah-wuh) 샤워
shrine	**sadang** (sah-dahng) 사당
shuttle bus	**shotul bosu** (shuttle bah-suu) 셔틀버스
sightseeing	**kugyong** (kuu-g'yohng) 구경 / **kwangwang** (kwahn-gwahng) 관광
signature	**somyong** (suhm-yuhng) 서명
silk	**pidan** (pee-dahn) 비단

singer	**kasu** *(kah-suu)* 가수
single room	**shinggul rum** *(sheeng-guhl ruum)* 싱글룸
sisters	**chamae** *(chah-may)* 자매
size (fit)	**saiju** *(sigh-juu)* 사이즈
ski	**suki** *(suu-kee)* 스키
ski resort	**suki rijotu** *(suuk-kee ree-joh-tuu)* 스키 리조트
sky	**hanul** *(hah-nuhl)* 하늘
sleep	**cham** *(chahm)* 잠
smoking area	**hubyon kuyok** *(huh-byun kuu-yuhk)* 흡연구역
snack	**kanshic** *(kahn-sheek)* 간식
snow	**nun** *(nun)* 눈
snowstorm	**nunbora** *(nun-boh-rah)* 눈보라
soldier	**gunin** *(guun-een)* 군인
South Korea	**Nam Han** *(Nahm Hahn)* 남한
souvenir	**kinyompum** *(kee-n'yohm-pume)* 기념품
speed limit	**chehan sokto** *(chay-hahn soke-toh)* 제한 속도
spicy (hot)	**maeun** *(may-uun)* 매운
sports	**undong** *(uun-dohng)* 운동
sprain	**ppida** *(beep-dah)* 삐다
sprained ankle	**palmogul ppiossumnida** *(pahl-moh-guhl pee-ah-ssume-nee-dah)* 팔목을 삐었 습니다
spring (season)	**pom** *(pome)* 봄
stadium	**undongjang** *(uun-dohng- jahng)* 운동장
staff (personnel)	**chigwon** *(chee-gwuhn)* 직원
star	**byol** *(b'yohl)* 별

steak	***suteiku*** *(su-tay-kuu)* 스테이크
stomachache	***poktong*** *(poke-tohng)* 복통
stop (halt)	***momchuda*** *(muum-chuu-dah)* 멈추다
stop (place)	***chungji*** *(chuung-jee)* 정지
street	***toro*** *(doh-roh)* 도로 / ***gil*** *(gheel)* 길
stroke (illness)	***choltto*** *(chohl-toh)* 졸도
student	***haksaeng*** *(hahk-sang)* 학생
suburb	***kyooe*** *(k'yoh-whay)* 교외
subway station	***chihachol yok*** *(jee-hah-chuhl yuhk)* 지하철역
sugar	***soltang*** *(sohl-tahng)* 설탕
suggestion	***amsi*** *(ahm-shee)* 암시
suit (law)	***sosong*** *(so-song)* 소송
summer	***yorum*** *(yoh-rume)* 여름
sunglasses	***songullasu*** *(sun-guh-lah-suu)* 선글라스
sweater	***suweto*** *(swea-tah)* 스웨터
swimming pool	***suyong jang*** *(suu-yohng jahng)* 수영장
swim suit	***suyong bok*** *(suu-yohng boak)* 수영복
system	***chegye*** *(chay-gay)* 체계
[T]	
table	***takcha*** *(tahk-chah)* 탁자
table tennis	***tak kut*** *(tahk kute)* 탁구
tailor	***yangbokjom*** *(yahg-boak-jome)* 양복점
Taiwan	***Taeman*** *(Tay-mahn)* 대만
tax	***segum*** *(say-gume)* 세금
taxi	***taekshi*** *(tack-she)* 택시

taxi stand	**taekshi sunggangjang** *(tack-she suhng-gahng-jahng)* 택시 승강장
teacher	**sonsaengnim** *(suun-sang-neem)* 선생님
television	**terebijon** *(tay-ray-bee-joan)* 테레비젼
temperature (weather)	**kion** *(kee-own)* 기온
terminal (domestic)	**kungnae chongsa** *(kuhng-nay chung-sah)* 국내 청사
text message	**munja** *(muun-jah)* 문자
Thanksgiving Day	**Chusok** *(Chuu-soak)* 추석
theater (movie)	**kukchang** *(kuhk-chahng)* 극장
theory	**iron** *(ee-roan)* 이론
thermometer	**cheongye** *(chohn-gay)* 체온계
ticket	**pyo** *(p'-yoh)* 표
ticket counter	**pyo panungot** *(p'yoh pah-nuhn-got)* 표 파는 곳
ticket vending machine	**pyo chapangi** *(p'yoh chah-pahn-ghee)* 표 자판기
tissue	**tishyu** *(tee-shuu)* 티슈
toast (bread)	**tostu** *(tos-tuu)* 토스트
toast (drinking)	**konbae haeyo** *(kom-bay hay-yoh)* 건배해요
today	**onul** *(oh-nuhl)* 오늘
toenail	**paltop** *(pahl-tohp)* 발톱
tomorrow	**naeil** *(nay-eel)* 내일
tonight	**onul chonyok** *(oh-nuhl chun-yuk)* 오늘 저녁
toothpick	**issushigae** *(ees-shu-she-gay)* 이쑤시개

tour (travel)	*tuo* (*tu-ah*) 투어
tourist	*yohaenggaek* (*yoh-hang-gake*) 여행객
traffic	*kyotong* (*k'yoh-tohng*) 교통
traffic light	*shinhodung* (*sheen-hoh-duhng*) 신호등
tranquilizer	*chinjongje* (*cheen-johng-jay*) 진정제
trash	*ssuregi* (*ssuh-reh-ghee*) 쓰레기
trash can	*ssuregitong* (*ssuh-reh-ghee-tohng*) 쓰레기통 / *hyujitong* (*hugh-jee-tohng*) 휴지통
travel	*yohaeng* (*yoh-hang*) 여행
travel agency	*yohaengsa* (*yoh-hang-sah*) 여행사
trousers	*paji* (*pah-jee*) 바지
truck	*turok* (*tuu-ruk*) 트럭
truth	*chilli* (*cheel-lee*) 진리
truth (fact)	*sasil* (*sah-sheel*) 사실
tunnel	*tonol* (*tuh-nuhl*) 터널
typhoon	*taepung* (*tay-puung*) 태풍
[U]	
umbrella	*usan* (*uu-sahn*) 우산
uncle	*samchon* (*sahm-chuhn*) 삼촌
underground passage	*chihado* (*jee-hah-doh*) 지하도
underground shopping center	*chiha sangga* (*jee-hah sahng-gah*) 지하 상가
unification	*tongil* (*tohng-eel*) 통일
uniform	*chebok* (*chay-boak*) 제복
university	*taehakkkyo* (*day- hahk-k'yoh*) 대학교
untrue	*kojishin* (*kuh-jee-sheen*) 거짓인

USA	*Miguk* *(Me-guuk)* 미국

[V]

vacancy (room)	*pin bang* *(peen bahng)* 빈 방
vacant	*pin* *(peen)* 빈
vacation	*hyuga* *(hyuu-gah)* 휴가; *bang hak* *(bahng hahk)* 방학
vaccination	*yebang* *(yay-bahng)* 예방
valid	*yuhyohan* *(yuu-h'yoh-hahn)* 유효한
valley	*koltchagi* *(kohl-chah-ghee)* 골짜기
valuables	*kwijungpum* *(kwee-juung-pume)* 귀중품
value	*kachi* *(kah-chee)* 가치
vegetarian	*chaeshikchuuija* *(chay-sheek-chuu- we-jah)* 채식주의자
vegetable(s)	*yachae* *(yah-chay)* 야채
vendor (seller)	*haengsangin* *(hang-sahng-een)* 행상인
view	*kyongchi* *(k'yohng-chee)* 경치
village	*maul* *(mah-uhl)* 마을
visa	*pija* *(bee-jah)* 비자
visitor (guest)	*sonnim* *(soan-neem)* 손님
vitamins	*bitamin* *(bee-tah-meen)* 비타민
voice mail	*umsong meshiji* *(uhm-suhng-may- she-jee)* 음성 메세지
volcano	*hwasan* *(hwah-sahn)* 화산
volleyball	*paegu* *(pay-guu)* 배구
voltage	*chon-ap* *(chone-ahp)* 전압
volume	*yang* *(yahng)* 양
vomit	*tohada* *(toh-hah-dah)* 토하다

[W]

wage	*imgum* *(eem-guhm)* 임금

wait (for)	*kidarida (kee-dah-ree-dah)* 기다리다
waiter	*weito (way-tah)* 웨이터
waitress	*weituresu (way-tuu-reh-suu)* 웨이트레스
walk (stroll)	*sanpo (sahn-poh)* 산보
wall	*byok (b'yuk)* 벽
wallet	*chigap (chee-gahp)* 지갑
watch (timepiece)	*shigye (she-gay)* 시계
waterfall	*pok-po (poak-poh)* 폭포
watermelon	*subak (suu-bahk)* 수박
waves (water)	*pado (pah-doh)* 파도
weapon	*mugi (muu-ghee)* 무기
weather	*nalssi (nahl-she)* 날씨
weather forecast	*ilgi yebo (eel-ghee yay-boh)* 일기예보
wedding	*kyorhon (kyuhr-hone)* 결혼
wedding anniversary	*kyorhon kinyomil (kyuhr-hone keen yuh-meel)* 결혼기념일
weigh	*muge-rul talda (muu-gay-ruhl tahl-dah)* 무게를 달다
weight	*muge (muu-gay)* 무게
west (direction)	*sotchok (suht-chock)* 서쪽
Western (cowboy movie)	*seobu yonghwa (say-buu yohng-hwah)* 서부 영화
wheat	*mil (meel)* 밀
whiskey	*wisuki (wis-kee)* 위스키
wholesale	*tomae (toh-may)* 도매
widow	*mimangin (me-mahng-een)* 미망인
widower	*horabi (hoh-rah-bee)* 홀아비
wife	*anae (ah-nay)* 아내
wind	*param (pah-rahm)* 바람
window	*changmun (chanhng-muun)* 창문

windy	***param punun*** *(pah-rahm puu-nuhn)* 바람 부는
wine (grape)	***podoju*** *(boh-doh-juu)* 포도주; ***wain*** *(wah-inn)* 와인
winter	***kyoul*** *(k'yoh-uhl)* 겨울
wireless	***musonui*** *(muu-suhn-we)* 무선의
world	***segye*** *(seh-gay)* 세계
wreck (destroy)	***pagoehada*** *(pah-gway-hah-dah)* 파괴하다
wrestling	***resulling*** *(ray-suhl-leeng)* 레슬링
wristwatch	***sonmokshigye*** *(sohn-moke-she-gay)* 손목시계
wrong (error)	***chalmot*** *(chal-mote)* 잘못
[XYZ]	
X-ray	***eks-rei*** *(x-ray)* 엑스레이
yacht	***yotu*** *(yah-tuu)* 요트
yard	***madang*** *(mah-dahng)* 마당
year	***hae*** *(hay)* 해
yesterday	***oje*** *(ah-jay)* 어제
young	***cholmun*** *(chuhl-muhn)* 젊은
zero	***yong*** *(yuhng)* 영
zipper	***chipo*** *(jee-pah)* 지퍼
zone (region)	***chidae*** *(chee-day)* 지대
zoo	***tongmurwon*** *(dohng-muhr-wuhn)* 동물원

ABOUT TUTTLE
"Books to Span the East and West"

Our core mission at Tuttle Publishing is to create books which bring people together one page at a time. Tuttle was founded in 1832 in the small New England town of Rutland, Vermont (USA). Our fundamental values remain as strong today as they were then—to publish best-in-class books informing the English-speaking world about the countries and peoples of Asia. The world has become a smaller place today and Asia's economic, cultural and political influence has expanded, yet the need for meaningful dialogue and information about this diverse region has never been greater. Since 1948, Tuttle has been a leader in publishing books on the cultures, arts, cuisines, languages and literatures of Asia. Our authors and photographers have won numerous awards and Tuttle has published thousands of books on subjects ranging from martial arts to paper crafts. We welcome you to explore the wealth of information available on Asia at www.tuttlepublishing.com.

Published by Tuttle Publishing, an imprint of Periplus Editions (HK) Ltd.

www.tuttlepublishing.com

Copyright © 2005, 2015 by Periplus Editions (HK) Ltd.

Library of Congress Cataloging-In-Publication 2004113424

ISBN 978-0-8048-4550-2

Distributed by

North America, Latin America & Europe
Tuttle Publishing
364 Innovation Drive
North Clarendon, VT 05759-9436 U.S.A.
Tel: 1 (802) 773-8930
Fax: 1 (802) 773-6993
info@tuttlepublishing.com
www.tuttlepublishing.com

Asia Pacific
Berkeley Books Pte. Ltd.
61 Tai Seng Avenue #02-12
Singapore 534167
Tel: (65) 6280-1330
Fax: (65) 6280-6290
inquiries@periplus.com.sg
www.periplus.com

First edition
20 19 18 17   4 3 2   1705CM
Printed in China

TUTTLE PUBLISHING® is a registered trademark of Tuttle Publishing,
a division of Periplus Editions (HK) Ltd.